SECOND EDITION

Toad
*Pocket Reference
for Oracle*

*Jeff Smith, Patrick McGrath, and
Bert Scalzo
Quest Software, Inc.*

O'REILLY®

Beijing · Cambridge · Farnham · Köln · Sebastopol · Tokyo

Toad Pocket Reference for Oracle, Second Edition

by Jeff Smith, Patrick McGrath, and Bert Scalzo

Published by O'Reilly Media, Inc., 1005 Gravenstein Highway North, Sebastopol, CA 95472.

O'Reilly books may be purchased for educational, business, or sales promotional use. Online editions are also available for most titles (*safari.oreilly.com*). For more information, contact our corporate/institutional sales department: (800) 998-9938 or *corporate@oreilly.com*.

Editor:	Deborah Russell
Production Editor:	Claire Cloutier
Cover Designer:	Ellie Volckhausen
Interior Designer:	David Futato

Printing History:

August 2002:	First Edition.
June 2005:	Second Edition.

ISBN: 978-0-596-00971-7
[LSI]   [2011-08-12]

Contents

Toad Pocket Reference for Oracle

Introduction

This book is a quick reference designed to help Oracle end users (data analysts, developers, designers, DBAs, etc.) become better users of Toad for Oracle. It is aimed at both beginning and experienced users. Clearly, given its small size, this book is not intended to be a comprehensive user's guide. Rather, it is a concise summary, designed to provide you with:

- A summary of the core functionality and major standard features available in the Toad for Oracle product
- A handy quick reference to common functions and short-cut keys, as well as recommended changes to default options
- A summary of helpful usage hints, tips, and cautionary notes

The material presented here applies to both commercial and freeware versions of Toad for Oracle.

TIP

The official name of the product described in this pocket reference is Toad for Oracle. For simplicity, we generally use the term "Toad," but unless specifically stated, that term refers to Toad for Oracle.

Toad is a constantly evolving product. It has had several upgrades each year since 1995. At the time this pocket reference went to press, the current version of Toad was Version 8.5. In order to be useful to as many users as possible, this book focuses on the product's continuing core functionality.

For more information about Toad go to:

http://www.quest.com

or:

http://www.toadsoft.com

For more information about this book, go to:

http://www.oreilly.com/catalog/tdpr2

Contributors

This book is a collaborative effort involving many individuals and groups—the dedicated members of the Toad Team, the Toad user community, and various resources at Quest Software, Inc. and O'Reilly Media, Inc.:

Jeff Smith
> Jeff was responsible for providing most of the technical updates for this edition of the book. He is a product specialist with Quest Software, Inc., responsible for Toadsoft.com, and is a liaison between customer support and the Toad Team.

Patrick McGrath
> Patrick is a senior systems sonsultant with Quest Software, Inc. He is the technical editor for various Oracle-related books.

Bert Scalzo
> Bert is a software architect for Quest Software, Inc., responsible for designing a number of product features, including many of those found in Toad.

Steve Hilker
> Steve is a senior product manager for the Toad Team at Quest Software, Inc.

Bryan Huddleston
> Bryan is the product marketing manager for Toad at Quest Software, Inc.

The Toad Team
> Toad is developed and maintained by an extraordinary band of developers, QA professionals, and tech writers. The entire team has taken on the Toad persona and adopted the Toad work ethic, elevating Toad to cult status within the Oracle community.

Thanks as well to the O'Reilly editorial and production team, especially to editor *par excellence* Debby Russell, and to others too numerous to mention who helped bring this book to life.

Caveats

This book assumes that you have a baseline familiarity with Oracle, PL/SQL, and SQL*Plus, as well as a basic understanding of Windows. In more advanced sections (e.g., "Database Administration"), we assume that you are a very experienced Oracle user.

We can't cover every possible Toad function in this pocket reference, but we do touch upon the key functions and windows available from every major section of the main Toad menus. There are a number of standard (and, for the most part, self-explanatory) Toad functions that we won't mention because of space limitations. In addition, a full description of Toad's add-on modules is beyond the scope of this small book; however, we do touch upon several optional features in the final section of this book.

For Help with Toad

In addition to this pocket reference, there are a number of other helpful Toad documentation resources available:

Toad Help files
> The Toad Help files cover every aspect of the product. Use the F1 key to access context-sensitive help for almost every Toad window and panel. Always check the "What's New" page for each Toad upgrade.

Toad product documentation
> Each Toad install includes the *Toad for Oracle User's Guide* and the *Toad for Oracle Getting Started Guide*. These two PDF files are located in the *Toad\docs* folder.

Toad FAQs
> Toad's Frequently Asked Questions are maintained and updated at:
>
> > *http://www.Toadsoft.com*

Toad user group
> Toad has an active online user group. You can subscribe by selecting **Help → Join Mailing Lists** and subscribing to:
>
> > *Toad-subscribe@yahoogroups.com*

TIP

Toad is a modular product. Check **Help → About** to determine your Toad version and verify which modules you have licensed. Certain features (e.g., the Project Manager, the SQL*Loader interface, etc.) are available only in Toad's commercial version.

Conventions

The following conventions are used in this pocket reference:

Italic
> Used for filenames, directory names, URLs, Toad options, and occasional emphasis

Bold
> Used for Toad menu choices

`Constant width`
> Used for code and command examples

`Constant width italic`
> Indicates that the item (e.g., a filename) is to be replaced by a user-specified value

→
> Used to indicate a menu choice; for example, **View → Options** indicates that you select View and then choose Options from the dropdown list

Toad Basics

What is Toad? Toad began as a development environment tool for Oracle. It has developed into a feature-rich program that provides a graphical user interface (GUI) to the Oracle database for all Oracle users. Using Toad will make you a more productive developer or DBA. The product makes program development faster and easier, and it simplifies database administration.

This section summarizes basic guidelines for using Toad. For detailed installation instructions, consult the previously listed Toad documentation sources.

Note the following Toad basics:

- In Toad, Oracle rules. Toad never violates, restricts, or enhances the Oracle privileges and permissions that have been defined for you. Toad does not affect your defined relationship to your Oracle instance in any way.
- Toad is closely integrated with Oracle. The Toad editor has the ability to execute nearly all SQL*Plus commands (except certain DBA commands such as STARTUP and SHUTDOWN).
- Toad has numerous window- and panel-specific right mouse menus. Check everywhere to see if a right mouse menu is available.

Installing and Configuring Toad

Toad has a wizard-driven installation with options for local, network, and Citrix installation. You will be prompted to choose options such as whether to use tabs or a tree-style Schema Browser, whether to run the Unix scheduler scripts, and so on. After the install is complete, you can always modify the default configuration from **View → Options**.

TIP

The basic Toad install does not require that any objects be installed in your Oracle instance.

Expanding Toad's Functionality

Once you have installed Toad, you can choose to expand its basic functionality by selecting **Tools → Server Side Objects Wizard**. This installs objects needed for running Explain Plans and using the Stored Program Profiler, Toad Security, and Team Coding facilities. You can install these objects into a selected schema or allow the wizard to create a Toad

---

schema to own the objects. The wizard will create and display a modifiable install script for these objects. Note that some of these selections may require DBA authority.

Configuring External Tools

You can configure Toad to open and execute external tools from the Configure button 🖫 on the Standard Toad toolbar (described later). The defaults include Notepad, Word-Pad, the SQL Monitor, and the SQL Optimizer.

Toad Startup and Other Options

Default settings are provided for all the major Toad windows. You should consider tuning these defaults to suit your own work environment. For example, you can select the Business Analyst, Developer, or DBA toolbar configuration, switch the default Startup window from the SQL Editor to the Schema Browser, or use an XP or enhanced display.

The following Toad startup options can be changed at any time. Changes in the options usually take effect immediately. You may find that you need to refresh windows that are active at the time these changes are made. If a particular change does not work for you, simply reset it. Startup options are available from **View → Options → StartUp** and **View → Options → Windows**:

Play Toad Wave File
> The Toad *.wav* file plays a "croak" when you open Toad and when you successfully compile a stored program. You can disable the Toad *.wav* file by unchecking this option. You can disable the croak following a stored program compile by unchecking *Notification when the compile process is complete* in **View → Options → Procedure Editor → General**.

Prompt for commit/rollback when changes detected, or detection is not possible due to lack of privileges on dbms_transaction

Checking this option in **View → Options → Oracle → Transactions** causes Toad to prompt the user to ROLLBACK or COMMIT any unposted transactions when closing an Oracle connection. Toad can determine whether there are valid transactions pending and can then prompt on exit only when necessary, assuming that the user has access to the SYS DBMS_TRANSACTION package. If the user does not have access, Toad will prompt for commit when closing any connection. There are also options for automatically committing and rolling back changes.

Confirm before closing Toad

If you turn on this option from **View → Options → General**, Toad forces you to answer the prompt "Are you sure you want to exit?" Before you turn this option off, though, remember that using it may save you from inadvertently closing Toad when all you intended to do was close a window.

Commit Automatically after every statement

Some users prefer to commit manually when needed rather than have Toad ask commit questions at the end of each Toad session. From **View → Options → Oracle → Transactions** you can configure Toad either to Auto-Commit after each statement or to not AutoCommit.

Window(s) to auto open at Startup

The SQL Editor, the Project Manager, and the General spool tab are opened at startup. Choose your appropriate startup window from **View → Options → Windows**. For example, for DBAs, opening both the Session Browser and the Database Browser may be a better choice.

Toad Properties Files

Options settings for Toad and Toad history files are stored in several different locations in your Toad folder.

Toad.ini

> Located in the *User Files* folder. Stores most of the information entered in **View** → **Options**. You can safely remove *Toad.ini* if you need to restore the default settings.

Connections.ini

> Stores all your connection information. (Note that connection history was stored in the *Toad.ini* file in previous versions of Toad.) If you choose the option to save your passwords, Toad stores them in an encrypted format.

Toad_GUI.ini

> Stores options that control your personalized Toad GUI (e.g., window size settings, and Session Browser GUI settings).

TopSess.ini

> Stores your list of profiles for the Top Session Finder.

SBQueries.dat

> Stores custom queries for the Schema Browser.

Toad_SESSBROWFILTERS.ini

> Stores all the canned and user-defined filters for the Session Browser. (This is the screen that replaces the Kill/Trace facility available in previous versions.)

Filecompare.ini

> Stores options for the Differences Viewer.

You can review the complete list of files in Toad Help under Properties Files.

Toad Menu Toolbar

The Toad Menu toolbar (Figure 1) currently has 13 menus.

Figure 1. Toad Menu toolbar

File

> Provides functions to open, save, reopen, and compare files; connect and test Toad connections to Oracle; perform FTP and network utility operations; execute scripts via the Script Manager; and run an archive function to zip files.

Edit

> Provides both standard text-editing functions and Oracle-specific functions (e.g., Columns Dropdown). This menu works with all three Toad editors (SQL Editor, Procedure Editor, and Text Editor), although the Oracle features are disabled for the offline Text Editor.

Grid

> Interacts with the **Schema Browser → Table/View → Data** tab and the **SQL Editor → Results Panel → Data** tab. Provides functions for searching, filtering, printing, and exporting the displayed data.

SQL Editor

> Provides functions for executing, saving, and recalling SQL statements, as well as functions to execute the SQL window via SQL*Plus or the Quest Script Runner.

Create

> Provides model dialog screens for creating Oracle objects such as DB links, policies, jobs, materialized views, users, resource plans, etc.

Database

Contains functions for opening the Schema Browser, the SQL Editor, the SQL Modeler, the Procedure Editor, and the Database Browser, as well as providing commit, rollback, import, export, and profiling functions.

Tools

Contains functions for Project Manager, ER Diagram, Compare Data, Code Road Map, SGA/Trace Optimization, Object Search, TKPROF Interface, etc. Also provides several DBA functions, including estimate, analyze, and rebuild utilities.

View

Provides the Explain Plan utility, Session Info, Reports, DBMS_OUTPUT window, the Object Palette, and Code Snippets. Also opens the Toad Options dialog.

DBA

Provides access to a number of utilities, including the Database Monitor, Session Browser, New Database wizard, expanded Export/Import utilities, Compare Schema/Database utilities, etc.

Debug

Interacts with the Procedure Editor to support a full set of PL/SQL debugging tools. You can set and manipulate watches and breakpoints, use various code execution options, etc.

Team Coding

Provides access to Toad's version control utility with Code Control Groups, Check In/Out, and other functions. Allows you to interface with SCC API source control products.

Window

Provides standard window functions such as Tile Vertical and Cascade, and displays your active windows in Toad for easy navigation.

Help

Provides access to Toad Help, as well as links to support at Quest Software, Inc. and to the Toad mailing lists.

Toad has predefined toolbars for developers, DBAs, and business analysts that are able to hide/display the appropriate menus and menu items for each group. These can be selected and modified from **View → Options → Toolbars/Menus**.

Toad Toolbar Display

The Toad Standard toolbar, shown in Figure 2, displays at the top of Toad's main window.

Figure 2. Toad Standard toolbar

The Toad Standard toolbar and several other Toad toolbars can be toggled on and off. Clicking the right mouse on the toolbar allows you to activate or deactivate your toolbars.

The Menu Shortcuts option displays the icons and their shortcut keys. You can define your own shortcut keys in this window.

SQL Editor

The SQL Editor, one of three editors available in Toad (along with the Procedure Editor and the Text Editor), is a full-featured editor, designed especially for working with Oracle databases and writing code for Oracle.

Display

The SQL Editor window is composed of a Script Navigation panel on the left, a tabbed Editing panel, and a multitabbed Results panel (described later in the "Using the Results Panel" section). You can toggle a full-screen display of the SQL Editor as follows:

F2
> Toggles a full-screen Editing panel

SHIFT-F2
> Toggles a full-screen Results panel

SQL Editor → Right Mouse → SQL Editor Desktop allows you to choose which Results panel tabs are visible (e.g., Query Viewer, Script Output, Script Debugger, Navigator, Explain Plan, DBMS Output, Data Grid, CodeXpert, and Auto Trace). You can also hide the Script Navigation panel.

Toolbars and Menus

The SQL Editor contains an extensive set of functions with multiple launch points, including menus, toolbars, shortcut keys, and right mouse menus. You can edit, execute, and debug statements and scripts from the Edit, Debug, and SQL Editor menus and toolbars.

In addition to Toad's Standard toolbar, there are several related toolbars: the SQL Editor Main toolbar, Standard (or Common) Edit toolbar, Formatting toolbar, Script Debugging toolbar, Source Control toolbar, SQL Recall toolbar, and Current Schema toolbar. The SQL Editor also has an extensive right mouse menu.

Toad's SQL Editor functions can be executed from several different locations to accommodate different user orientations (some users prefer the mouse, others the keyboard; some like toolbars, others prefer menus). For example, you can execute SQL in your editor by pressing F9, by clicking the Execute SQL All button on the Edit toolbar, or by selecting **SQL Editor → Execute SQL All**.

TIP

Not all functions are available in all locations. Some functions are available from only one source; for example, the "Add to Named SQLs" function can be selected only from the SQL Editor menu (there is no predefined shortcut key for this function).

Main toolbar

The SQL Editor Main toolbar contains buttons for executing statements, generating explain plans, changing the active session for the SQL Editor, launching the Tuning Lab, and opening and saving files. The Main toolbar also displays a Cancel button for long-running queries and data scrolls in the data grid.

Edit toolbar

The Standard (Common) Edit toolbar is common to the SQL Editor and the Procedure Editor. It also appears in a somewhat modified fashion in the Text Editor. Standard editing features—such as cut, copy, paste, search, search and replace, undo, etc.—should be self-explanatory. The functions that make a non-SQL code statement and that strip all non-SQL syntax are located next to the Print button.

Formatting toolbar

The Formatting toolbar contains buttons for formatting and for profiling your code.

Script Debugging toolbar

The Script Debugging toolbar contains functions that let you run a script, step over statements one at a time, set and toggle breakpoints, and run to a cursor. (See the "Use the Script Debugger" section for more information.)

Source Control toolbar

The Source Control toolbar has functions that allow you to get the latest version from source control, check in to or out from source control, undo checkout, add to source control, and select the active project. (See the "Source Control" section for more information.)

SQL Recall toolbar

The SQL Recall toolbar pulldown lists your currently defined Named SQLs, giving you easy access to saved SQL statements. (See the "Invoke SQL Command Recall" section for more details.)

Current Schema toolbar

The Current Schema toolbar is available only if you have the ALTER SESSION privilege. Behind the scenes, it executes ALTER SESSION SET *current_schema* = *schema_name* statements prior to execution of the editor contents. After execution is complete, another ALTER SESSION SET *current_schema* statement is issued to return the current schema back to the schema assigned to the SQL Editor. This operation applies to explain plans and executed SQL. It does not have an effect on any execution run via the Script Engine (that is, F5 or "Execute as Script").

Use the Set Schema function to resolve any *ORA-00942, Table does not exist* errors you receive when you have unqualified table names in your statements and scripts. Choose the appropriate Set Schema value, and your query will work in Toad.

TIP

The Change Session function switches SQL Editor execution ownership to any other user that exists in the connected instance. Set Schema does not require that you open a new connection for the "qualifying" owner.

SQL Editor menu

The SQL Editor menu (shown in Figure 3) shares certain SQL execution options with the SQL Editor Main toolbar. You can execute a single SQL statement, a highlighted statement, or an entire script. There are foreground and background execution functions available, and it has the ability to describe (parse) a SELECT query. You can also save statements as either Personal or Named SQLs.

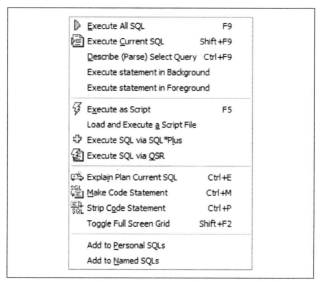

▷	Execute All SQL	F9
	Execute Current SQL	Shift+F9
	Describe (Parse) Select Query	Ctrl+F9
	Execute statement in Background	
	Execute statement in Foreground	
⚡	Execute as Script	F5
	Load and Execute a Script File	
	Execute SQL via SQL*Plus	
	Execute SQL via QSR	
	Explain Plan Current SQL	Ctrl+E
	Make Code Statement	Ctrl+M
	Strip Code Statement	Ctrl+P
	Toggle Full Screen Grid	Shift+F2
	Add to Personal SQLs	
	Add to Named SQLs	

Figure 3. SQL Editor menu

Edit menu

The Edit menu (shown in Figure 4) includes many of the usual editing features: undo, redo, cut, copy, paste, find, replace, etc.

This menu also provides a number of Oracle features for describing the object at the cursor, displaying a column name list for the table or view at the cursor, and displaying procedure arguments. The menu provides functions for alias

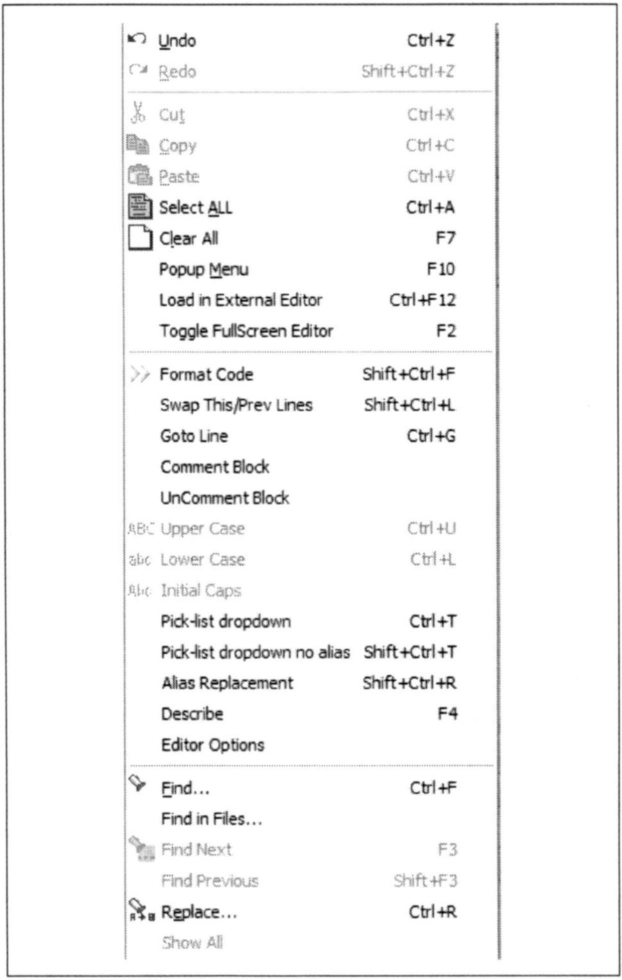

↶ Undo	Ctrl+Z
↷ Redo	Shift+Ctrl+Z
✂ Cut	Ctrl+X
📋 Copy	Ctrl+C
📋 Paste	Ctrl+V
📋 Select ALL	Ctrl+A
📄 Clear All	F7
Popup Menu	F10
Load in External Editor	Ctrl+F12
Toggle FullScreen Editor	F2
≫ Format Code	Shift+Ctrl+F
Swap This/Prev Lines	Shift+Ctrl+L
Goto Line	Ctrl+G
Comment Block	
UnComment Block	
ABC Upper Case	Ctrl+U
abc Lower Case	Ctrl+L
Abc Initial Caps	
Pick-list dropdown	Ctrl+T
Pick-list dropdown no alias	Shift+Ctrl+T
Alias Replacement	Shift+Ctrl+R
Describe	F4
Editor Options	
🔍 Find...	Ctrl+F
Find in Files...	
🔍 Find Next	F3
Find Previous	Shift+F3
🔍 Replace...	Ctrl+R
Show All	

Figure 4. Toad Edit menu

replacement and for loading an external editor. The Show All function shows all the results from the Find function.

Right Mouse menu

SQL Editor → Right Mouse menu provides access to additional text manipulation, execution trace, and Editor display functions. Using this menu (shown in Figure 5), you can set bookmarks for easy navigation through long scripts. You can also change blocks to all uppercase, lowercase, or initial caps. Comment Block and UnComment Block functions are available, as are functions to create PL/SQL's DBMS_OUTPUT statements, apply Unix-style file saves, select the different Oracle optimizer modes (not available in Oracle Database 10g connections), and initiate Oracle's SQL Trace (TKPROF) or Toad's AutoTrace programs in order to gather Oracle execution statistics. (See the V$ Tables Required page in Toad Help for the tables needed to access the optimization screens.)

Shortcut Keys

The SQL Editor provides a useful set of shortcut keys, which are listed in Table 1. Note that these shortcut keys are specific to the SQL Editor. They are available in both the Editing panel and the Results panel.

There is a fair amount of shortcut key definition duplication among the various Toad editors (SQL Editor, Procedure Editor, and Text Editor). However, there are also significant differences. For example, the shortcut F9 executes a statement in the SQL Editor, but it compiles a stored program in the Procedure Editor.

Toad allows you to customize shortcut keys in the SQL Editor, Procedure Editor, and Text Editor. You can make your modifications by selecting **Edit → Editor Options → Key Assignments**.

As we mentioned, some menu options and toolbar buttons do not have a predefined shortcut key. You define shortcut keys for those options by right-clicking over the Toad Standard toolbar and choosing Menu Shortcuts.

Figure 5. SQL Editor Right Mouse menu

Table 1. SQL Editor shortcut keys

Shortcut key	Function
F1	Windows Help for current window
F2	Toggle full-screen Editing panel
SHIFT-F2	Toggle full-screen Results panel

Table 1. SQL Editor shortcut keys (continued)

Shortcut key	Function
F3	Find next occurrence
SHIFT-F3	Find previous occurrence
F4	Describe highlighted table, view, procedure, function, or package in pop-up window
F5	Execute as script
F6	Toggle active window between SQL Editor and Results panel
F7	Clear all text in SQL Editor, Data tab, and Explain Plan tab
F8	Recall previous SQL statement in SQL Editor (full history view)
F9	Execute statement in SQL Editor
CTRL-F9	Verify SELECT statement without execution (parse) in SQL Editor
SHIFT-F9	Execute statement at cursor in SQL Editor
F10	Pop-up menu
CTRL-F12	Load in external editor
CTRL-A	Select all text
CTRL-C	Copy
CTRL-E	Execute Explain Plan on the statement or on the highlighted statement
CTRL-F	Find text
CTRL-G	Go to line number
CTRL-L	Convert highlighted text to lowercase
CTRL-M	Make code statement
CTRL-N	Recall named SQL statement
CTRL-O	Open a file for editing
CTRL-P	Strip code statement
CTRL-R	Find and replace
CTRL-S	Save file
SHIFT-CTRL-S	Save file as
CTRL-T	Specify column dropdown for highlighted table, view, or synonym
CTRL-U	Convert highlighted text to uppercase

Table 1. SQL Editor shortcut keys (continued)

Shortcut key	Function
CTRL-V	Paste
CTRL-X	Cut
CTRL-Z	Undo last change
SHIFT-CTRL-Z	Redo last undo
ALT-UP	Display previously executed statement (single statement view)
ALT-DOWN	Display next statement (after ALT-UP in single statement view)
CTRL-HOME	In the data grids, go to the top of the record set
CTRL-END	In the data grids, go to the end of the record set
CTRL-TAB	Cycle through the open windows in Toad
CTRL-ENTER	Execute current statement (same as Shift-F9)
CTRL-(period)	Autocomplete table name, view, or synonym after initial characters have been typed
ALT-PgUp/PgDn	Navigate the editor panels
CTRL-ALT-PgUp/PgDn	Navigate the output panels

Supporting Other Parsers/Languages

While the SQL Editor recognizes only Oracle's PL/SQL language, the Procedure Editor and the Text Editor can parse text from other languages such as HTML and Java. These editors recognize the language you are using by the extension of the file loaded.

Go to **View → Options → Parser Scripts** to configure support for other languages. To configure options for Toad's parser scripts, go to **Edit → Editor Options**.

The filenames for the parser of a given language, such as HTML, all start with the name of that language (for example, *htmlscr.txt, htmlkeys.bin, htmlopts.txt, html.dci*).

Working with Files in the SQL Editor

This section describes ways to open and work with files using the SQL Editor.

Open files

There are several ways to open a file in the SQL Editor:

File → Open File
> You can open an existing file located in your Windows network via this function from the Toad Menu toolbar. (Remember that you can use **File → Reopen Files** to access previously opened files.)

Main Edit Toolbar → Open File
> You can click on the "Open File" button on the Main Edit toolbar.

CTRL-O
> You can type CTRL-O in any editor to open a Load File window.

Integrated Source Control/Team Coding

Toad supports the Source Code Control (SCC) standard, a Microsoft API that defines a standard interface between development environments and source control products. The SCC API provides functions that perform common source control operations.

With Toad's Source Control toolbar, you can check in or check out files to/from Microsoft Visual SourceSafe, PVCS, and other source control programs. You need to have the client portion of the source code control application installed on your PC. Alternately, you can use Toad's Team Coding, which is discussed in the "Procedure Editor" section, later in this book. While not all SCC-compliant products have necessarily been tested, all such products should work with Toad. For more detailed information read the "Team Coding and SCC Interaction" Help topic.

Make the appropriate entries in **View → Options → Team Coding** so Toad recognizes your installed version control software. You will need to provide Toad with your default working directory. Set the appropriate options for checkin and checkout prompts, and for comments when new files are added. Each file will open in its own tab in the SQL Editor.

Executing Statements

Toad allows you to execute statements in several different ways. You can execute statements one at a time, execute all of the content in the SQL Editor at once, or execute the content in the SQL Editor as a script.

Execute all SQL

The SQL Editor provides functions that allow you to execute single SQL statements. This may be a standalone statement, a highlighted statement, or a statement executed as a script. The tabbed format includes both the Editing panel and the Results panel so that each tab acts like a standalone SQL Editor.

The SQL Editor can handle both query statements and DDL statements. For example, enter the following statement on the first SQL Editor tab:

```
SELECT * FROM tablename WHERE rownum < 50
```

Toad does not require semicolons to terminate SQL statements.

There are several other ways to execute a SQL statement. You can select **SQL Editor → Execute All SQL**, click on the Execute All SQL button on the SQL Edit toolbar, or press F9. Your execution results will display on the Data tab in the Results panel (see the "Using the Results Panel" section).

Execute a single statement

The SQL Editor can execute a single statement from within a series of statements, as in a script, as long as they are separated by at least one blank line or a line with a '/. Click or place the caret/cursor within the desired statement or on the blank line after the statement you want to execute. Then press SHIFT-F9 or CTRL-ENTER, or click the "Execute statement at cursor" button on the toolbar to execute the statement at the cursor.

Execute a script

The SQL Editor can also execute multiple statements as a script as long as they are terminated by semicolons. For example, enter the following statements in a SQL Editor tab:

```
SELECT * FROM scott.emp;
SELECT * FROM scott.dept;
SELECT * FROM user_tables;
```

To execute the contents of your editor as a script, you can select **SQL Editor → Execute as Script**, click on the "Execute as Script" button on the Script Debugging toolbar, or press F5. The SQL Editor's Script Engine is invoked to execute each statement. If Toad encounters an error, it will ask you if you want to continue or terminate the script.

The Script Output tab will show all of the script execution results in the Output subtab. Also, each executed statement that returns at least two cells (e.g., SELECT 1,2 from dual) will have a Grid subtab. These tabs will display the results returned in each statement in a data grid. Thus, if your script contains five SELECT statements, your Script Output tab will have one Output subtab and five Grid subtabs.

Execute SQL*Plus

Although the SQL Editor can execute many of Oracle's SQL*Plus commands, some of these commands are either ignored or not supported. If your SQL contains SQL*Plus commands that are not supported in the SQL Editor (see the upcoming tip), select **SQL Editor → Execute SQL via SQL*Plus**. Toad opens a SQL*Plus connection in an independent window using your current Toad/Oracle login. Your SQL will be executed immediately without further prompting.

You can then arrange your desktop to take advantage of the SQL Editor for editing statements or full scripts by copying and pasting them into the SQL*Plus window.

TIP

Remember to add the final semicolon (;) before attempting to execute Toad's SQL Editor window in SQL*Plus.

Search on SQL*Plus in Toad Help for the list of SQL*Plus commands currently supported by the SQL Editor.

Execute with ScriptRunner

Quest ScriptRunner (QSR) is a small script-execution utility that can be used to edit and execute DDL and DML scripts. You might run such scripts in the background while working on other tasks on your desktop. QSR is not 100% SQL*Plus compatible; however, most DDL and DML scripts should be supported. QSR does provide single-step execution, as well as the ability to run to a cursor and run from cursor execution. QSR is available from **SQL Editor → Execute SQL via QSR**.

Quest ScriptRunner can be run from the executable or from the command line, giving you flexibility in how you schedule and run scripts.

Parse (Describe) a SELECT statement

Toad has the ability to parse a SELECT statement, and report on which columns will be returned, without having to execute it. Type any single SELECT statement, such as the following, in the SQL Editor:

```
SELECT * FROM tablename WHERE ROWNUM < 50
```

Instead of immediately executing the statement, you can parse the statement either by pressing CTRL-F9 or by selecting **SQL Editor → Describe (Parse) Select Query**. Oracle will treat the statement as "describe only." The resulting window displays the column names, datatypes, and data lengths of all of the columns that will be returned by the query.

If you misspell a column name, or if that column no longer exists, the query will not parse completely but will stop at the invalid column name.

Use substitution variables

Toad opens the Variables input window when you execute a statement using bind variables in the SQL Editor. When you execute the following:

```
SELECT * FROM EMPLOYEE WHERE employee_id = :EMPID
```

you will be prompted to select the datatype and enter your value before clicking OK to continue execution. Toggling *Scan statements for bound variables before execution* in **View → Options → SQL Editor → General** will disable this.

Cancel running statement

Toad lets you cancel long-running queries. When a statement such as the following is executed:

```
SELECT * FROM DBA_OBJECTS ORDER BY object_id
```

the Cancel button at the right end of the Execute function on the SQL Edit toolbar is active as long as the query can be terminated.

Using Extended Features

This section briefly describes some more advanced features available from the SQL Editor.

Use the Script Debugger

This extended Toad feature is available only in Toad for Oracle editions that include debugging functionality. The Script Debugger is an extension to the SQL Editor that you can use to debug SQL scripts. You can load multiple scripts; each will open in its own tab (consult Toad Help for more information). In addition to standard SQL Editor functions, the following functions are available from the Script Debugger:

- Set Breakpoints
- Run to Cursor
- Step Over
- Trace Into
- Halt Execution
- Start Execution from Cursor (useful when a script has partially executed and encounters an error; you can fix the error and start execution from that point)

The Script Debugger output panel displays all of your SQL environment variables and their values, lists breakpoints in your scripts, and displays a call stack during your debugging session.

Invoke SQL Command Recall

View → SQL Command Recall F8 displays a dockable window that stores your previously executed statements (100 by default; 999 maximum) from the SQL Editor for easy reuse. Press F8 to recall the full list of saved statements. SQL statements are saved in the file *Toad\User Files\SAVEDSQL.xml*. The older statements age out as you continue to execute new statements. Multiple executions of the same statement create one entry in the *SAVEDSQL.xml* file, but the Last Execution timestamp is updated. The *SAVEDSQL.xml* file is maintained between Toad sessions. You can increase the number of statements saved under **View → Options → SQL Editor → SQL Recall**. You can also set the option to *Save Only statements that are valid*, which is the default setting starting with Toad Version 8.5.

The SQL Recall window has various operation buttons and display options in its Main and SQL filtering toolbars. These buttons and options let you navigate through the list and select and delete statements from it. You can group your

SQL history by SQL type or by connection, and edit the stored SQL in the SQL Recall window. Statements can be changed from temporary "History Items" to "Saved Items" by clicking in that column. The Named SQL dropdown menu will populate as you name your History items. There is also a "SQL Contains" search available from this window. When you are searching for a SQL statement with a unique text string in it, use the "SQL Contains" dialog to filter out all of the statements that don't contain that text string.

Display Object Palette (tables, views, synonyms, columns)

View → Object Palette displays a dockable window that shows all the tables, views, and synonyms for a schema. The Object Palette can also display the columns and associated datatypes for each object. You can drag-and-drop any item from the list into the SQL Editor or the Procedure Editor. (Finding the item in the list verifies that the object currently exists in the database and helps eliminate misspellings.) Double-click on the object name to paste it in the SQL Editor at your cursor position. When you select multiple object names to drag-and-drop into the SQL Editor, Toad inserts them as a comma-separated list.

Use the Show Columns button on the Object Palette toolbar to display the columns for the highlighted object. The column panel has the same drag-and-drop capabilities as the Object window.

Display code snippets

View → Code Snippets displays a window that can be pinned or docked. Code snippets include Oracle date, group, single-row character, and single-row number functions. The window is divided into upper and lower panels; functions are listed in the upper panel, and the description of the highlighted function is displayed in the lower panel. You can drag-and-drop the displayed functions directly into the SQL Editor window or perform the same action by double clicking.

TIP

You can modify code snippets by editing the appropriate *FUNCS.TXT* files in the *Toad\User Files* folder. There is a specific section for your own SQL templates labeled "User Provided Function List", which you can populate by editing the *USRFUNCS.TXT* file in the *Toad\User Files* folder.

Use **SQL Editor** → **SQL Command Recall F8** for storing and reusing single-line SQL statements. This window is not intended for storing full SQL statements. Another set of templates, available through **Edit** → **Editor Options** → **Code Templates**, allows you to store and reuse multiple-line code statements and templates. Use the **File** → **Script Manager** utility for handling multiple-script storage and execution.

Change Active Sessions for this Window

Toad supports multiple simultaneous connections to the same (or different) Oracle instances with the same (or different) Oracle logins. When you need to execute a statement or a script on an Oracle instance that is different from the one to which you are currently connected, or if you want to run it as a different owner, click on the "Change Active Session for this Window" button at the far right on Toad's Standard toolbar. If you already have other Toad sessions active, they display, along with the option to open a new session. The new session opens at your current active window instead of using your default startup window.

TIP

When you click on the "Change Active Session for this Window" button, you can navigate between your current session and your new session. Toad displays your login name and your instance name at the top and bottom of each window. Look for this button on most of Toad's other window toolbars as well.

Make a Non-SQL Code Statement/
Strip All Non-SQL Syntax

The "Make a Non-SQL Code Statement" and "Strip All Non-SQL Syntax" buttons let you add development code syntax to SQL statements or remove it from the statements in the SQL Editor. These buttons are located on the SQL Edit toolbar.

With a single, valid SQL statement in the SQL Editor, or a highlighted statement and the appropriate code development language (Delphi, VB, C++, Java, or Perl) selected in **View → Options → SQL Editor → Make Code**, click on the "Make a Non-SQL Code Statement" button. Alternately, press CTRL-M. This adds the development code to your statement and copies it to the clipboard. Toad displays an appropriate message, such as "Java statement copied to the clipboard," in the status bar at the bottom of the SQL Editor window.

To reverse the action and remove development code from your statement, copy the SQL from your development code into the SQL Editor. Then highlight it and click on the "Strip All Non-SQL Syntax" button. Alternately, press CTRL-P.

TIP

You can add/edit existing code or add new language templates in **View Options → SQL Editor → Make Code**.

Use the EDIT command

As an alternative to executing an updateable SQL statement, consider using the Toad EDIT command when you need to update, insert, or delete data for a table. For example, the command:

```
EDIT tablename F9
```

is equivalent to running:

```
SELECT tablename.*, ROWID FROM tablename
```

Both commands return all the data from the specified object in updateable mode. The red gem display, indicating "Read Only", changes to a green gem, meaning that you are now in Updateable mode. The Data Edit buttons ("Insert a row", "Delete a row", "Post data changes", and "Revert data changes") on the SQL Edit toolbar also become active while the data grid is in updateable mode.

Use the Toad Describe facility

The Toad Describe facility opens an extended Describe for Oracle database objects. It provides much more detailed output than does the SQL*Plus DESCRIBE command.

The Toad Describe opens a multitabbed window that displays the schema name, column names, datatype, data, grants, script, etc., for the described object. You can drag-and-drop column name(s) into the SQL Editor from this window. Double-clicking on the column name generates a comma-separated list. You can also check Oracle's currently enforced referential integrity, the current status of constraints and triggers, and the current data. In addition, you can see the other Oracle objects (views, snapshots, procedures, etc.) that use the described object by clicking the appropriate tab.

Execute the Toad Describe facility by typing:

```
DESC objectname F9
```

The Toad Describe has a predefined shortcut key, F4, which you can press while your cursor rests on the object name.

TIP

Toad Describe is actually the Object Details panel from the Schema Browser (see the "Schema Browser" section later in this book). The Describe functionality is available from all of the Toad editors, and you can even use F4 in some of the other Toad screens.

Display column dropdown

Toad can display a list of columns for a table or view. Type the object name in the SQL Editor, followed by either a period or CTRL-T, as shown here:

```
tablename.
tablename CTRL-T
```

The column dropdown list is also available as a menu item. Position your cursor at the desired table name and select **Edit → Column Dropdown**. You can select column names from the displayed list.

Use code templates

Toad comes with approximately two dozen default code completion templates for SQL operations (e.g., entire cursor block, package spec cursor, function shell). These appear in a popup menu that is common to the SQL Editor, the Procedure Editor, and the Text Editor. You can open the Code Completion Template popup by pressing CTRL-Spacebar. You can also bring the code into the editor by typing its shortcut followed by CTRL-Spacebar. For instance, if you type:

```
Crbl CTRL-Spacebar
```

Toad opens the SQL template for declaring a cursor block (Crbl) in the editor. You are then prompted to enter the appropriate values.

In addition to using the default templates, you can create your own templates with positions marked for table names and other substitutions by selecting **Edit → Editor Options → Code Templates**. In addition to creating templates in the editor, you can use the "Load from File" button at the bottom of the window to load your previously defined files and formats into Toad's code completion templates.

The source for Toad's code completion templates is the *PLSQL.dci* file in your Toad *User Files* folder.

Format code

Toad's built-in formatter lets you format the entire contents of the SQL Editor. Toad can format a single, valid SQL statement, a series of statements, or an entire script (including comments). With your code displayed in the SQL Editor, select **Right Mouse → Formatting Tools → Format Code**.

You can customize formatting from **View → Formatting Options**.

TIP

If your code fails to format properly, look at the SQL Editor's status bar and check your code for syntax errors.

Add and remove comments

Toad provides a convenient method for adding comments to, and removing comments from, your code. These functions are available from **Edit → Comment Block** and **Edit → UnComment Block** as well as from **Right Mouse → Comment Block** and **Right Mouse → UnComment Block**. The functions are available in the SQL Editor, the Procedure Editor, and the Text Editor.

Toad "comments out" a highlighted section of a displayed script in the SQL Editor by adding a double dash to the beginning of each line.

Data Grid

The powerful data grid Toad provides is an integral part of the product's success. Traditional Oracle SQL*Plus result sets are brought back as static text—often requiring extensive FORMAT commands to get something that resembles readable results. On the other hand, Toad's data grids are instantly readable, are easily accessible, and allow for many different exportable formats.

Manipulating the Display, not the Query

Once you are satisfied with your SQL query, you are ready to work with your query's result set. You can execute the statement once and then view many possible different permutations of your data's formats, layouts, and even content. SQL*Plus limits you to one result format; changing the layouts and columns available requires you to rewrite and re-execute your query.

Sort data, rearrange columns, and filter data

With Toad's data grid, you can reorder the result set's columns by simply dragging and dropping the column headers to the desired location. You can easily hide/unhide columns by selecting **Right Mouse → Select Columns** on the grid. If you are interested in only viewing a subset of the data, you can filter the data by clicking on the column header drop-down button and selecting Custom. Figure 6 shows an example of using Excel-style filtering on the grid (the option must first be activated, as described in the next section).

A single left-click on a column header in the data grid opens a dialog to apply or remove an ascending or descending sort on that column. When the operation is complete, the data grid refreshes. A pointer displayed in the column header indicates the direction of the sort.

You can remove the sort using the same left-click on the column header in the data grid. If you wish, you can also remove the sort confirmation when clicking on column headers by going to **Options → Data Grids → Visual** and deselecting *Confirm sorts when clicking on column header*.

Configure data grid options

The Toad data grid provides many different display and data handling options. For example, you can configure the grid to autosize the columns based on either the length of the column name or the width of the column data. To customize

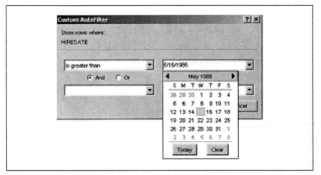

Figure 6. Excel-style filtering

your data grid settings, either select **Right Mouse → Grid Options** from any data grid or proceed to **View → Options → Data Grids**. You will see the available options.

There are two sets of data grid options (Data and Visual). These options are common to all Toad grids, so any changes to them are reflected in the SQL Editor, Schema Browser, and almost anywhere else you are presented with a data grid. There are a few exceptions, most notably the grids presented in the Script Output tab of the SQL Editor.

Here are a few Data options you may want to customize:

Default to Read Only Queries
Forces your grids to be read-only. Selecting this option can prevent unintended data changes.

Stop data fetches when available memory becomes less than n MB
Specify a value for *n*; the default is 12 MB. When the specified limit is reached, Toad stops the data scroll to prevent your system resources from being consumed.

Here are some customizable Visual options:

Row Select
Enables you to select an entire row at a time as opposed to a single cell.

Row Numbers Enabled
> Enables you to display row numbers in your result sets.

Multi Select
> Enables you to select multiple rows of data. Selecting this option facilitates exporting subsets of data and copying/pasting data in your grids.

Allow Excel style filtering
> Enables you to filter the contents of your result set.

Navigating the Grid

The data grid is a fairly straightforward object that is very easy to navigate. However, there are a few things to keep in mind while using it that will make your data-browsing experience more enjoyable.

Scroll down

When retrieving data from Oracle, Toad receives the data in blocks. When you scroll down through the result set, Toad will ask Oracle for more of the data. The amount that Toad receives for each fetch is configured in **View** → **Options** → **Oracle** → **General** in the option:

OCI Array Buffer size number box
> This option lets you set the size of the OCI Array buffer You can set the buffer to a maximum value of 999. The disadvantage of choosing a higher setting is that Toad must allocate memory to hold that many rows prior to each fetch. If that many rows are actually fetched, there is no loss. On the other hand, if not that many rows are retrieved, then some memory is allocated that will not be released until the cursor is freed. This amount of allocated memory is generally unnoticeable. The default for this option is 25.

When you have executed your query, or when you have selected a table to browse in the Schema Browser, the rows you see in the data grid are the ones that Toad has received from its initial fetch. If you pull the scrollbar down to the bottom, this will ask Toad to retrieve *all* the records. For large result sets, this can be a very memory-intensive operation. Toad may appear to freeze, but it is actually bringing back all the records and constructing the grid contents to allow you to browse the data.

Scroll left to right

When you are viewing datasets that contain many columns, it can be quite frustrating to have to scroll back and forth to be able to view the particular information you want. Toad's data grid allows you to "fix" a column or group of columns. Anchoring a column on the lefthand side of the data grid can make it easier to track information when you are doing a lot of scrolling.

To anchor a column, click in a column to select it. Then right-click and select Fix Column to fix the selected column. The selected column is anchored to the left. To move a column out of the fixed area, click and drag it to the right of the bold fixed-column divider bar.

Editing Data from the Data Grid

Toad's advanced data editors simplify the updating of your data. No more remembering the proper TO_DATE or TO_CHAR functions for your INSERT/UPDATE/DELETE statements! For you to edit data via the data grid, the result set must be editable. There are several ways to achieve an editable result set (the status is displayed in the data grid panel with either a green or a red gem):

- Do a SELECT that returns the ROWID (Toad requires the ROWID in order to update the record).
- Use Toad's EDIT command (for example, use "edit employee" instead of SELECT EMPLOYEE.*, ROWID FROM EMPLOYEE).

- Browse the data from the Schema Browser where the result set defaults to editable status. Don't forget to check the *Default to Read Only Queries* option discussed in the earlier section "Configure data grid options."

Toad's data grid employs data-specific editors that allow easier editing of specific datatypes. The following list shows which editor or editing function you can use for each datatype:

Datatype	Editor/Function
BLOB	Upload a File, or Save the contents to a file
BFILE	Custom Popup Editor
CLOB	Advanced Text Editor
CHAR, VARCHAR, CLOB, or LONG	Advanced Text Editor
INTEGER, NUMBER, DOUBLE, FLOAT, BINARY_DOUBLE, BINARY_FLOAT	Calculator
DATE/INTERVAL/TIMESTAMP	Calendar
Nested tables	Custom Popup Editor
User-defined objects	Custom Popup Editor
XML	XML Tree Editor

You can also quick-edit a row by typing directly into the cell; this is convenient for smaller textual fields. For large text or advanced datatypes like XML, you can invoke the Popup Editor by selecting **Right Mouse → Popup Editor** or by double-clicking on the cell. The datatype displays in the grid as "(*datatype*)," as shown for "ORAXML" in Figure 7.

When you have finished making your changes, be sure to post the changes using the "Post edit" button on the Popup Editor toolbar. This will send your changes to Oracle. You can then COMMIT or ROLLBACK your session.

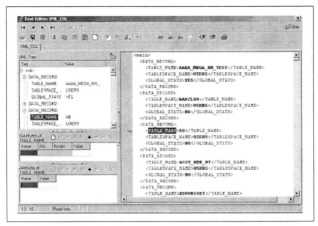

Figure 7. Popup Editor for a XML datatype

Access the Single Record View

You can access the Single Record View by clicking on the book icon in the upper left of the data grid. The Single Record View window opens and displays your current record on a single panel. This view reflects any sorting and filtering of data and any hiding or reordering of columns that have been set in the data grid. Many users appreciate being able to use the option *Sort columns in record view dialog* available from **View** → **Options** → **Data Grids** → **Data** to sort their columns for this view.

Saving/Sending Data in Various Formats

Once you have assembled, sorted, and filtered your data, you will have numerous output functions available to you.

The Save As function is available both from the Grid menu on the Toad Menu toolbar and from any Toad data grid's

Data → Right Mouse menu. You can choose to save the data in the data grid in a number of different formats by selecting these options:

- Delimited Text (you choose the delimiting character)
- Fixed Field Spacing
- HTML Table
- Insert Statements
- SQL Loader
- XLS File (Excel)
- XLS Instance (Toad creates an Excel file within the current Excel instance running on your machine)
- XML (plain)
- XML (with XSL)

As you change formats, you may notice that additional options appear for those formats—for example, NULL text, Zip Resulting file(s), and file or clipboard destination.

The data exported by the Save As function is not limited to the rows displayed in the data grid. All rows of data resulting from your query are saved to either the clipboard or a file (depending on which target you have selected). Your saved data is sorted, filtered, excluded, and otherwise manipulated based on your display manipulations and the options you select in the Save Grid Contents window.

Earlier in this chapter we mentioned the *Multi Select* option for the data grids available from **Visual → Options**. If you have enabled this option, then you will be able to export selected rows via the Save As dialog. Highlight the rows you want exported, then enable the *Selected rows only?* option in the Save As dialog.

Schedule a Save As

You will notice on the Save As dialog a "Save Options to File" button. This button allows you to generate a text file with all of the options specified in the dialog. You can use this file to schedule Toad to save a query's results or a data grid's contents to a file. Read the commented section in the generated file for more details.

Display Record Count from right mouse grid popup

Most of the data grid functions should be self-explanatory. One that may require some clarification is Record Count, which counts all the records returned by a query (note that this function is not limited to counting the records displayed in the data grid). With your data displayed in the data grid and your cursor in the Results panel, select **Right Mouse → Record Count**. (Figure 8 shows the right mouse menu.)

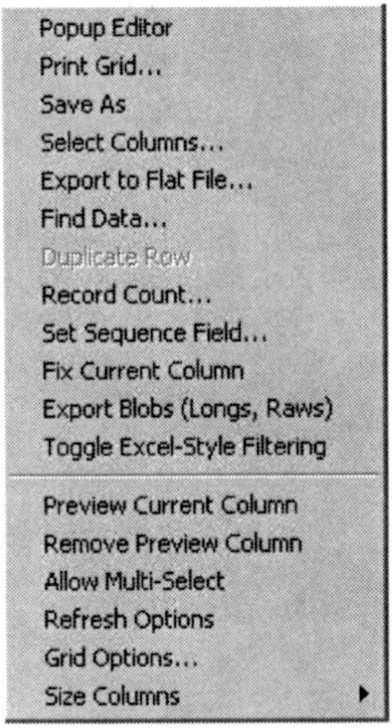

Figure 8. Right mouse grid popup menu

Print Grid engine

The Print Grid feature may also require some explanation. Toad offers two different Print Grid engines. You select the one you want to use from **View** → **Options** → **Data Grids** → **Data** via the option:

Use the older version of the Data Print Grid
> When checked, this tells Toad to use the old Toad Print Grid dialog box. If unchecked, Toad uses the newer Report Link Designer (this is the default).

Working with Data

Toad has many different utilities for making data manipulation less of a chore. This section briefly discusses four of the most powerful ones. For more detailed information, consult Toad Help or the *Toad for Oracle User's Guide*.

Master Detail Browser

You can use the Master Detail Browser window to view or edit data from multiple tables in which foreign keys link the tables. For example, you could start with the DEPARTMENT table, pick "EMPLOYEE" from the related table's dropdown list, and select a department record; the employee records will be displayed only for that department. There is a static limit of five related tables that you may have open in the browser at one time.

The Master Detail Browser is accessible via **Tools** → **Master Detail Browser**.

Compare Data wizard

You can use Toad's Compare Data wizard to compare data between tables within different schemas or different databases. This can be useful for comparing the data found in a production and test environment, for example. Toad allows you to configure the datasets you wish to compare (e.g., selecting the columns, ordering the data, specifying optimizer hints for faster queries). Once the comparison report has been generated, you can view the differences. For example, you can:

- Review rows in Source 1 that are not in Source 2
- Reviews rows in Source 2 that are not in Source 1
- Review all differences

The Compare Data screen is accessible via **Tools → Compare Data**.

Import Table Data wizard (from text file or Excel)

When you're dealing with relatively small amounts of data, it sometimes does not make sense to take the time to generate a custom SQL*Loader control file—especially if you are not comfortable with SQL*Loader in the first place. Toad offers a wizard that allows you to import data from a text file or a Microsoft Excel spreadsheet into an existing table. The Import Table Data wizard is accessible from **Database → Import**.

The wizard allows you to:

- Select the schema and table from which you want the data imported
- Perform one commit after all records, commit after each record, or do not commit
- View the existing table data and truncate it if desired
- Enable/disable constraints
- Enable/disable triggers
- Map the raw data fields to the destination table columns

TIP

Datasets to be loaded must be small enough to fit in memory. For large datasets, convert your data to a text file (if it is not already a text file) and use the SQL*Loader wizard (available with Toad's DBA Module.)

Table Data Duplicates window

Oracle users often must perform data cleanup on tables without the proper constraints—for example, tables without Primary or Unique constraints on the appropriate columns. Or perhaps you want to create a Unique constraint, but Oracle will not allow it because of table duplicates. Select **View →** **Table Data Duplicates** to select a table, find duplicate rows for specified columns (or all), and edit the offending data.

SQL Optimization

Toad provides a number of tools for manually identifying and optimizing poorly running SQL—for example, statements that are CPU- or I/O-intensive. These tools include:

- Explain Plans that show how Oracle executes a statement
- Several functions for reviewing statistics after statement execution, including Explain Current SQL, SGA/Trace Optimization, and the Session Browser.
- Toad for Oracle Xpert Edition with complete automated SQL optimization

Explain Plans

EXPLAIN PLAN is an Oracle command that analyzes a SQL statement for performance without actually executing the statement. The purpose of this command is to determine before execution the plan that Oracle will follow when optimizing and executing a SQL statement. The results of the EXPLAIN PLAN command display the order in which Oracle will search/join the tables, the types of access that will be employed (indexed search or full table scan), and the names of indexes that will be used. The display is read from the deepest indentation out.

Explain Plan in the SQL Editor

In the SQL Editor, you can generate an EXPLAIN PLAN command before executing a valid SQL statement by clicking on the "Run Explain Plan for current statement" button (the ambulance) on the SQL Edit toolbar. You can also press CTRL-E to generate the plan.

The generated plan displays on the Explain Plan tab available from the Results panel. If you wish, you can display this information from the right mouse menu. The "Run Explain Plan for current statement" function is also available in the SQL Modeler.

Toad expects to find an Explain Plan table with columns matching the most recent specification from Oracle. If you get Invalid Column errors when executing Explain Plan, check in the *ToadPREP.sql* script for the columns you may be missing. The Toad Explain Plan table is backward-compatible with earlier Oracle releases.

You can set the name of the Explain Plan table in the **View** → **Options** → **Oracle** → **General** window. Adjust the information in the dialog and enter your Schema and Explain Plan table name.

Previous Explain Plan results

Toad stores previously generated Explain Plans for review and comparison. You can access these from **View** → **Explain Plan** or by clicking on the "Show Previous Explain Plan Results" button (the ambulance button with the blue line above it) on the Toad Standard toolbar.

The resulting multipaneled Explain Plan window displays previously generated plans. You can compare the generated plans for variations of the same queries, different queries, and so on. This window does not have any editing capabilities, so if you decide to make changes to the displayed SQL statement, you must do so in the SQL Editor. Once you have made these changes, you can generate a new Explain Plan while in the SQL Editor and then return to the Explain Plan window and click the Refresh button to update the display.

You may occasionally need to perform some maintenance to clear Explain Plan results that are no longer needed. Select the obsolete Explain Plan results and click Clear.

Before you can use the Previous Explain Plan Results feature, you must go to **View → Options → Oracle → General** and turn on the *Save previous Explain Plan results (requires Toad tables)* option.

SQL Optimization Facilities

The following sections describe a variety of Toad facilities used to review statistics and tune SQL statement execution.

AutoTrace

Toad's AutoTrace feature lets you review resource usage for a particular query in the SQL Editor. AutoTrace is a mini-version of Oracle's SQL Trace (described in the next section). AutoTrace requires that the query be generated in order to capture execution statistics.

AutoTrace displays information such as Recursive Calls, Physical Reads, Consistent Gets, Index Scans, etc. The results are displayed in the AutoTrace tab of the Results panel.

If AutoTrace is not enabled when you click the AutoTrace button in the Results panel, Toad prompts you to enable it. You can enable or disable AutoTrace from **SQL Editor → Right Mouse → AutoTrace**. Once enabled, AutoTrace remains enabled until you disable it or the Toad session is terminated.

SQL Trace (TKPROF)

SQL Trace (TKPROF) is a server-side Oracle trace utility that
captures CPU, I/O, and resource usage during statement execution. SQL Trace is a much more complete utility than
AutoTrace. The output file is created on your Oracle server
in the directory specified in the USER_DUMP_DEST parameter of your *INIT.ora* file. You can view this file from **Tools
→ TKPROF Interface**.

The TKPROF wizard-driven interface prompts you for the
trace file(s) you want to view, lets you choose sort options
and data elements to view, and then displays the results in a
separate window.

To enable the TKPROF interface, select **View → Options →
Executables**. If the path for your TKPROF executable is not
identified, click on the flashlight icon to have Toad locate the
path for you.

SGA Trace Optimization

You can use the **Tools → SGA Trace Optimization** function
to view information about SQL statements that have been
executed and the resources they used. Whereas AutoTrace
and TKPROF information is specific to a single statement,
SGA Trace Optimization displays statistics from multiple
SQL statements currently present in Oracle's System Global
Area (SGA).

Go to **Tools → SGA Trace Optimization** to open the SGA
Trace window. You can set several options from this screen
in order to search for SQL statements. The default settings
are for "ALL Statements" for "ALL Users", but you can click
on the corresponding dropdown box and choose other

options to change these choices. You can limit the selection to a single statement type (e.g., SELECT statements, UPDATE statements, anonymous PL/SQL, etc.) or to a specific user. You can also enter a text string in the SQL Search Text box to limit the rows returned to statements containing that text string.

Click on the "Refresh the List of Statements" button to retrieve the most resource-intensive SQL from the SGA. This returns all of the queries that match your criteria. The screen is divided into two parts:

Top half
> The query results grid on the top half of the screen shows the query that was executed and the associated resources used (memory, disk reads, loads, etc.).

Bottom half
> The bottom half of the screen displays the full SQL statement, execution statistics from the Oracle shared pool, and the Explain Plan for the query.

When necessary, you can pass a SQL statement into the SQL Editor from the SGA Trace window. Highlight the desired statement, then click on the "Load selected statement in a SQL Editor" button on the SGA Trace toolbar.

This toolbar also contains a button to "Flush the SGA". Your Oracle privileges dictate your logged-in user's ability to use this function.

TIP

Tools SGA Trace Optimization requires access to a number of Oracle V$ objects. For a current listing of the Oracle access required to utilize this feature, go to **Help →
Contents**. From the Table of Contents, select **Toad Basics → V$ Tables Required**.

Session Browser

Selecting **DBA** → **Session Browser**, like **Tools** → **SGA Trace Optimization**, requires access to a number of Oracle V$ objects.

The Session Browser window allows you to view, work with, and manage sessions. You can organize session views based on filter and group criteria and view detailed information about sessions (including blocking locks and transaction information for online rollback segments, kill sessions, and start/stop traces).

The Session Browser default is laid out in two vertical panes: the left contains a treeview of the grouping, filtering, and sessions, and the right contains details about the session.

Sessions can be grouped and filtered based on user requirements. You can group sessions by selecting the appropriate options from the dropdown menu. You can filter sessions by creating a user-defined filter or selecting the filter button and selecting one of the static filters: Exclude NULL and SYSTEM OS Users, or Exclude parallel slaves.

When necessary, you can selectively kill sessions using the Kill Sessions function from the toolbar. The ability to kill a session is governed by the logged-in user's Oracle privileges.

Selecting "Start trace for this session" from the toolbar enables traces for selected user sessions. Selecting "End trace for this session" disables traces for these sessions.

The Session Browser has full support for running against RAC instances. When RAC is detected, this screen's information will be gathered from the appropriate GV$ tables. You will simply note the addition of an extra column in grid outputs for the instance ID. Moreover, this screen is aware of the current connection's instance versus the instance of a requested operation, and will autoconnect to the proper instance, perform the task, and then disconnect—all without requiring you to do anything.

Additional Tuning Methods

In addition to the manual methods, Toad provides an add-on module, Quest SQL Optimizer for Oracle, which provides a number of tools for automatically identifying and optimizing poorly running SQL. The SQL Optimizer is included with the Toad for Oracle Xpert Edition. These tools include:

SQL Scanner
Identifies the SQL statements that need to be tuned and ranks every SQL statement according to suspected levels of performance problems.

SQL Optimization/SQL Rewrite
Generates all SQL statement variations that are semantically equivalent to the source SQL, finding every possible alternative execution plan and the highest performing SQL.

Index Expert
Identifies the index set that yields the highest performance gain by generating every possible new index scenario for a given SQL statement.

Best Practices/Advice
Verifies SQL against a set of expert rules and advises on how to correct any problems found.

The details of these tools are beyond the scope of this book; refer to the Toad documentation for insights and instructions on using them.

Schema Browser

Toad's Schema Browser allows you to browse the contents of your database, providing a quick view of the objects in the database. The Schema Browser separates the objects shown in Figure 9 into separate tabs.

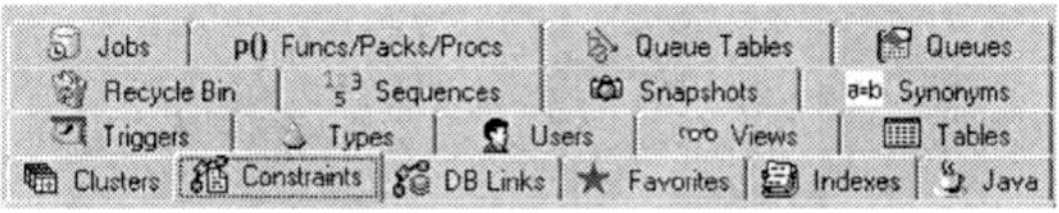

Figure 9. Schema Browser tabs

The additional tabs shown in Figure 10 are available with the optional DBA Module.

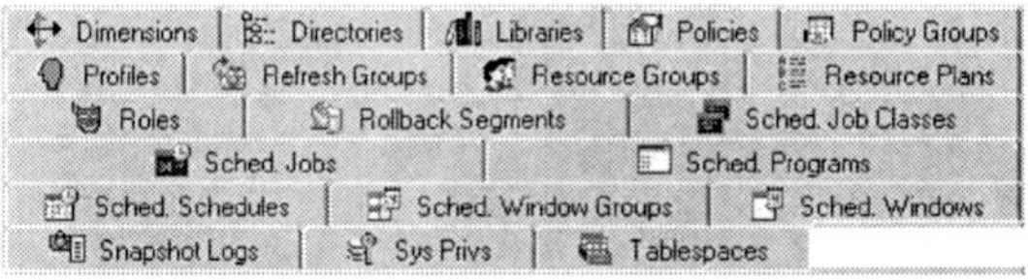

Figure 10. Schema Browser tabs available with DBA Module

Once you select an object type, the Schema Browser displays information on the objects in that category on the lefthand side of the browser window in an area known as the Objects panel. When you click on an individual object on the lefthand side, details for that object are displayed on the righthand side of the browser window in a separate area known as the Details panel. This display eliminates the most common complaint about treeview-based object browsing— the constant need to drill down through hierarchical mountains to find the desired data.

Configuring the Schema Browser

You can take advantage of various options for configuring the Schema Browser in order to suit your own needs.

Visual options

As you can tell from looking at the list of the object tabs in the figures above, there are quite a few objects to navigate.

While most users may like the default tabular navigation, others may prefer a different display interface. The Schema Browser has three display modes:

- Tabs (multiline and scrolling single line are available)
- Dropdown list
- Treeview

You can also configure the Schema Browser to display the object types in the order you choose. The labels themselves are even customizable. For example, if you find the Procs tab label confusing, you can rename it "Functions | Procedures | Packages". Here are the Visual options we recommend you evaluate before you spend much time in the Schema Browser.

For **View** → **Options** → **Schema Browser** → **Visual**:

Browser Style, Tabbed, Dropdown, Treeview
    This style can also be changed dynamically from within the Schema Browser. On the righthand side, use the Options button on the Schema Browser toolbar.

Show Left Hand Side Tab/Dropdown Icons
    Toad has a visual representation of each object type in the object selector. Disable this if you want more display room for the lefthand side of the browser.

Behavioral and data-specific options

If you will be interacting with very large databases, you'll also want to investigate the Schema Browser Data options. Certain settings can impact performance. Here are the options we recommend you evaluate.

For **View** → **Options** → **Schema Browser** → **Data**:

Omit SYS objects from the Procedure Dependencies List
    Omits SYS-owned objects from the Procedure Dependencies list—for example, the standard packages DBMS_STANDARD, DBMS_UTILITY, and so on.

Save filters for LHS lists
> Saves your browser filters (specific to each schema) between Toad sessions.

User Schema Lists
> Allows you to filter the contents of the User/Schema dropdown/tab to show *only* schemas that own objects. This can make it more manageable to browse objects in a database that has hundreds of schemas created only to enforce security. You can further filter this list to show only users that own objects *not including* synonyms. If you do not see all of your schemas as expected in the Schema Browser, review the setting for this option.

For **View** → **Options** → **Schema Browser** → **Data and Info Grids**:

Save Data Grid Layouts
> Remembers the data grid filters, column reordering, and visible columns for all grids between Toad sessions.

Enable FK Lookup in data grids
> When you are editing a record, pulls up all of the child records for a column that has a Foreign Key constraint. For very large lookup tables, Toad's performance may be adversely affected.

Limit Grid Fetch
> If a value, n, is entered, fetches only n x 25 results to the SQL results grids at a time. This option applies to the Tables Data and the Views Data tabs.

Only show top-level grants for Users, Roles, Sys Privs, and Resource Groups tabs
> Shows only the grants that have been directly granted to the user. Checking this option greatly improves the loading time of these Schema Browser tabs, but clearing it gives you a detailed view of which privileges a user/role has been given.

Use NOPARALLEL hint in data grids
Uses the NOPARALLEL hint in the data grids, making the queries consume less of Oracle's resources when displaying data from tables that have parallelism.

Objects Panel

As mentioned previously, the lefthand side (LHS) of the Schema Browser displays the Objects panel (an example is shown in Figure 11). When you specify an object type in the Tab/Dropdown/Treeview selector, the Schema Browser lists all of the objects of that type for the schema selected. The Schema Browser defaults to the login schema for the current session.

Toad checks your Oracle version and displays or suppresses Schema Browser tabs accordingly. For instance, the Schema Browser does not attempt to report on policies or libraries when connected to an Oracle 7.x database (which does not support such objects).

The Schema Browser lets you create, alter, copy, drop, export, enable, disable, compile, and perform a variety of other actions on the objects you select. Note, however, that the current Oracle privileges of the logged-in user determine which actions you are allowed to perform. These privileges also affect your ability to display and alter objects owned by other schemas.

An Oracle schema could be composed of many thousands of objects per object type. The Schema Browser allows you to filter the objects list in the Objects panel using the Filter button on the LHS Schema Browser toolbar.

Objects panel toolbar

The buttons available on the LHS toolbar depend on the object type selected. There are several buttons that appear for most object types:

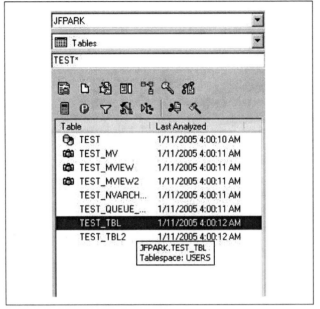

Figure 11. Objects panel (LHS of Schema Browser)

Filter (object type)

Allows the user to apply a filter on the objects that appear on the LHS.

Create (object type)

Opens the Create dialog for the selected object type.

Alter this (object type)

Opens the Alter dialog for the selected object.

Drop selected (object type)

Drops the selected object(s).

Create Public Synonym

Creates a public synonym for the selected object.

View/Edit Privileges for this (object type)
Opens the Privileges window for the selected object. Allows you to view, grant, and revoke privileges on a database object. You can view all users and their privileges.

Create Script
Generates the selected object(s) data definition language (DDL). You can configure the DDL options, including the output formats (Clipboard, File, Screen).

Objects panel right mouse

You will realize the full power of the Schema Browser only by exploring the right-click operations available for each of the Schema Browser object types. All of the Schema Browser toolbar operations are also available on the right-click menus. In addition, the following operations are available only from the right-click menus:

Add to Project Manager
Adds the object to your current project for the appropriate schema.

Add to SB Favorites List
Adds the object to your Schema Browser Favorites tab (see the next section).

Compare with another Object
Brings up the Compare Schemas functionality for the selected object.

Create in another schema
Automatically generates the DDL for the object for any connection/schema.

Create Like
Similar to "Create in another schema", but allows you to select *any* schema for your current connection.

Custom Queries

Allows you to create quick custom queries from the Schema Browser. The query will be built with your selected objects and placed into the SQL Editor for editing or running.

Favorites tab

The Favorites tab allows you to group different types of objects that you use frequently into a tab on the Schema Browser. These different objects can be grouped into one or several *folders*. A folder is maintained at the instance level: folders are specific to an instance (not to a connection or a schema).

Objects supported in this window include tables, views, PL/SQL code (procedures, functions, packages, triggers), and files.

TIP

The Favorites page is not available in the treeview of the Schema Browser.

If you appreciate the Favorites tab, make sure to investigate the Project Manager (discussed in the later "Project Manager" section) as well, as it has even more powerful grouping capabilities.

Details Panel

As mentioned previously, the righthand side (RHS) of the Schema Browser displays the Details panel. When an item is selected on the LHS panel, Toad displays information for that item above the RHS toolbar (shown in Figure 12).

BIGNUMBERS: Created: 12/14/2004 10:00:19 AM Last DDL: 12/14/2004 10:00:19 A

Figure 12. Details panel (RHS of Schema Browser)

Here you can see that a table named BIGNUMBERS has been selected from the Objects panel on the LHS of the Schema Browser. The Details panel on the RHS displays the time the object was created and the last time an ALTER command was executed against it. Slightly different information will appear depending on the object type selected.

The RHS toolbar contains the following functions, invoked from the icons shown in the figure:

Item History
> Provides quick navigation shortcuts for the objects you have browsed.

Refresh ALL Lists
> Refreshes all the lists in both the Objects panel and the Details panel.

Refresh Objects Panel
> Refreshes only the data in the Objects panel.

Refresh Details Panel
> Refreshes only the data in the Details panel.

Clear All Data Grid Filters
> Resets all filters in the Schema Browser in the current Toad session.

Icon Legend
> Deciphers the images presented in the Schema Browser.

Browser Style
> Allows you to dynamically switch the Schema Browser display style (TAB | DROPDOWN | TREE).

Select Session
> Selects a session for the current window.

In addition to the main RHS toolbar, there are toolbars for selected RHS tabs. For example, if you have selected object type "Users" on the LHS Objects panel, then the RHS tab toolbar for System Privileges lets you expand/collapse the privilege lists, revoke privileges,etc.

Schema Browser Tips and Tricks

Here are some suggestions for using the Schema Browser to your best advantage:

- Double-click an object on the LHS to alter it. Right-click to do just about anything else with it.
- Drag-and-drop an object into a Toad editor for faster querying.
- Use Toad Security to disable the Truncate and Drop buttons.
- If the object is present in a label on the RHS of the Schema Browser, you can describe the object or jump to the object:
  - To describe the object, click on the object label.
  - To jump to the object, hold down CTRL and click.
- If the object is present in an information grid on the RHS of the Schema Browser, you can describe the object or jump to the object:
  - To describe the object, press F4 on the object label.
  - To jump to the object, hold down SHIFT and press F4.
- To make more room for information, disable the Show LHS Images function from the browser-style RHS toolbar.
- Use the LHS QuickFilter box to filter the object list without having to requery the database.
- Right-click on the LHS header to enable the Schema | Tablespace | Last Analyzed columns for your objects.
- Enable the LHS filtering option *Search in All Schemas* to show all database objects in a single list.

Procedure Editor

Toad's Procedure Editor is designed to make editing, compiling, and executing stored programs as easy as possible. The Procedure Editor and the SQL Editor have many functions in

---

common; the overlap between them includes both traditional editing and Oracle-specific editing functions. However, the Procedure Editor provides many specific features that facilitate the handling of different types of stored programs such as procedures, functions, packages, types, and triggers. These features include specialized navigation, the entering and saving of parameters, program execution, the use of the DBMS_OUTPUT package, and so on. The Procedure Editor allows you to create new stored programs, work with existing stored programs, or work with files.

You can access the Procedure Editor in many different ways. The two most direct ways are to:

- Click on the "Procedure Editor" button on the Toad Standard toolbar
- Select **Database → Procedure Editor**

In both cases, the Procedure Editor then opens an empty editor window.

Procedure Editor Options

Many of the options that Toad allows you to customize have an impact on the Procedure Editor. These range from adding the owner when extracting source from the database to limiting Toad to one Procedure Editor per database connection. This section summarizes the options we recommend you customize; they are available via **View → Options → Procedure Editor**.

In addition, many of the editing options for the SQL Editor also apply to the Procedure Editor. See the discussion of the **Right Mouse → Editing Options** and the **Edit → Editor Options** in the "SQL Editor" section, earlier in this book. These options are common to all Toad editors, so any changes to them are reflected in the SQL Editor, the Procedure Editor, and the Text Editor.

*Use "CREATE" instead of "CREATE OR REPLACE" when
loading database objects*
> Available from **View** → **Options** → **Procedure Editor** →
> **General**. Consider whether it is more appropriate for
> your work environment to use CREATE instead of CRE-
> ATE OR REPLACE (the default) when loading database
> objects.

Load Spec and Body as a pair (Package or User Type)
> Available from **View** → **Options** → **Procedure Editor** →
> **General**. This option will force loading of the specifica-
> tion and body of a package or a type whenever one is
> opened.

Procedure Editor, Auto open
> Available from **View** → **Options** → **Windows**. If you
> anticipate spending much of your time in the Procedure
> Editor, consider changing the Procedure Editor to your
> default Toad startup window.

Configuring the Procedure Editor

Toad provides many options for configuring and customiz-
ing the Procedure Editor to meet your editing needs. The
Right Mouse → **Procedure Editor Desktop** menu lists
options to display or hide the Navigator panel, the Debug
Output panel, and the Status toolbar. Also, the various toolbars (Edit, Main Procedure Edit, and Debug) are customizable from this menu.

Procedure Editor Display

The default Procedure Editor window is divided into two
vertical panels; additional panels appear when necessary:

Navigation panel
> This panel always displays on the left. It shows the
> desired declarations within your code. (See the discus-
> sion later in this section for more details.)

Code-Editing panel

This panel always displays on the right. It displays the code for your currently loaded object. Multiple objects are split into separate Editor Tabs. The Tab label indicates the object it contains.

Errors panel

This panel opens across the bottom of the Procedure Editor window when errors are encountered during compilation. The appropriate PLS or ORA error and its description display in this panel. At the same time, the line where the error was detected is highlighted in the Code-Editing panel. (See the later section "Procedure Editor → Right Mouse" for more information.)

Output panel

If you have the add-on Toad Debugger module installed, a dockable Debug Output panel (with tabs for Breakpoints, Watches, DBMS_OUTPUT, Call Stack, and REF CURSOR Results) displays in the lower-right panel. (See the discussion in the "Debugger" section, later in this book.) The add-on CodeXpert module also has a tab in this panel. (See the discussion in the later section "Additional Toad Modules.")

The Navigation panel lets you view the constants, cursors, exceptions, parameters, records, record fields, REF cursors, subtypes, and variables declarations in your code. By default, all of these types of declarations are displayed. The Navigation panel places your cursor at the beginning of any declaration displayed in the Code-Editing panel when you click on its navigation item.

Procedure Editor Keys

If you prefer to use keyboard keys to navigate through the Procedure Editor, use the following:

CTRL-PgUp
 To move *up* through the Navigator panel

CTRL-PgDn
 To move *down* through the Navigator panel

ALT-PgUp
 To move *right* through the Editor tabs

ALT-PgDn
 To move *left* through the Editor tabs

CTRL-ALT-PgUp
 To move *right* through the Debug Output panel tabs

CTRL-ALT-PgDn
 To move *left* through the Debug Output panel tabs

Procedure Editor Menus and Toolbars

The Procedure Editor displays several toolbars, described in the following sections. In addition, a right mouse menu is available from the Procedure Editor.

Procedure Edit toolbar

The Procedure Edit toolbar is the second toolbar displayed in the Procedure Editor. Functions for "Compile", "Check in/ Check out from source control", "Load source from existing object", "Create new PL/SQL object", and so on are displayed here.

Debugger toolbar

If you have the optional Debugger module installed, the Debugger toolbar is displayed at the right end of the Procedure Edit toolbar.

Formatter toolbar

Formatting and CodeXpert functionality is accessible from the Formatter toolbar.

Right Mouse menu

The **Procedure Editor** → **Right Mouse** menu (shown in Figure 13) offers more than two dozen functions. Some functions are standard editing functions, and some you may recognize as duplications from the SQL Editor's right mouse menu. However, a number of functions, such as "Compile" and "Execute without Debugging", are unique to this right mouse menu. Most are self-explanatory.

The Procedure Editor lets you work on several stored programs at one time; each is loaded on a separate, labeled tab. Use the New Tab and Close Tab functions available from **Procedure Editor** → **Right Mouse** to govern these operations.

Populating the Procedure Editor

You can populate the Procedure Editor with existing stored programs from your Oracle instance or from script files. These can be accessed in a number of ways.

There are load options on the Toad Menu toolbar, as well as various choices on the Procedure Editor toolbar, for loading from files or from existing sources in your Oracle database. Objects can be loaded using:

- The Load File button on the Procedure Edit toolbar
- The "Load Source from an existing object" button on the Procedure Edit toolbar

First select the appropriate schema/owner. Then select objects from groupings of any of the following: procedures, functions, complete packages, package specs, package bodies, complete types, type specs, type bodies, and all stored programs. A preview panel displays your code for review before loading it in the Procedure Editor.

You can load stored programs from the Schema Browser. Once the object is highlighted, select **Right Mouse** → **Load** in the Procedure Editor.

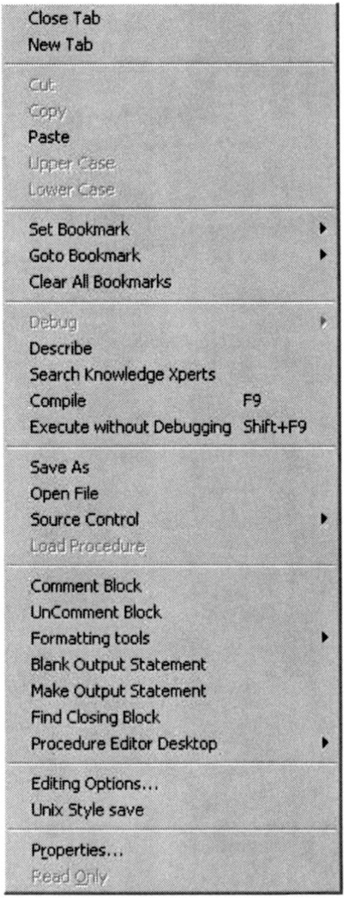

Close Tab
New Tab

Cut
Copy
Paste
Upper Case
Lower Case

Set Bookmark   ▶
Goto Bookmark   ▶
Clear All Bookmarks

Debug   ▶
Describe
Search Knowledge Xperts
Compile   F9
Execute without Debugging   Shift+F9

Save As
Open File
Source Control   ▶
Load Procedure

Comment Block
UnComment Block
Formatting tools   ▶
Blank Output Statement
Make Output Statement
Find Closing Block
Procedure Editor Desktop   ▶

Editing Options...
Unix Style save

Properties...
Read Only

Figure 13. Procedure Editor right mouse menu

Procedure Editor Shortcut Keys

The Procedure Editor provides a set of shortcut keys that you can use instead of selecting options from the various editing menus. Table 2 lists the available keys. Note that these keys are specific to the Procedure Editor's Code-Editing panel although many are shared by Toad's other editors.

Table 2. Procedure Editor shortcut keys

Shortcut key	Function
F2	Show/hide Errors panel
F4	Describe object under cursor in popup window
F5	Set or delete breakpoint on the current line
CTRL-F5	Add watch at cursor
SHIFT-F7	Trace into
SHIFT-F8	Step over
F9	Compile
SHIFT-F9	Execute without debugging
CTRL-F9	Set parameters
F10	Display right mouse menu
SHIFT-F10	Trace out
F11	Run (continue execution)
F12	Run to cursor position in Code-Editing panel
CTRL-ALT-B	Display breakpoints
CTRL-ALT-D	Display DBMS_OUTPUT
CTRL-ALT-E	Evaluate/modify
CTRL-ALT-S	Display call stack
CTRL-ALT-W	Display watches
CTRL-Mouse click	Move to the selected package procedure

Using the Procedure Editor

The following sections describe various Procedure Editor functions and operations that may not be self-explanatory.

Customize Toad templates

When the Procedure Editor opens, it displays a blank, untitled tab used for entering a new program from scratch. Alternately, you can load and manipulate source from a file or an existing program. You can also use the default Toad templates for a new procedure, function, package, trigger, or type.

From the Procedure Editor toolbar, click on the "Create New PL/SQL" button. This opens the New Procedure Create Options window, where you enter the new object name. Then select the appropriate object type (e.g., procedure) from the dropdown list.

All Toad new object templates are stored as SQL files in the *Toad for Oracle\User Files* folder. The templates are defined through **View → Options → Procedure Editor → Proc Templates**. You can edit these files according to your local standards, or you can create your own custom templates.

Create output statements

Toad provides a quick utility for creating DBMS_OUTPUT. PUT_LINE statements. Selecting **Right Mouse → Blank Output Statement** creates a "DBMS_OUTPUT.PUT_LINE (' ');" statement and copies it to the clipboard.

In addition to creating blank output statements, Toad can use the value of a variable that you enter to produce a complete output statement. Position your cursor on a variable name and select **Right Mouse → Make Output Statement**. The variable name is included in the statement created in the clipboard, as follows:

```
DBMS_OUTPUT.PUT_LINE ( 'variable_name= ' || variablename)
```

Use Code Completion

Toad's editors can help you write code much faster using code completion shortcuts. For example, Toad can resolve your package members if you place a period (".") after the package name. For example, to see all of the DBMS_OUTPUT functions and procedures available, type "DBMS_OUTPUT." in the editor. Toad will "pop up" all of that package's members. You can then scroll through the list and select the member you wish to call. Toad can also resolve column names for views and tables.

Use DBMS_OUPUT package

TIP

This section applies to the DBMS_OUTPUT package in the Procedure Editor. This is handled differently if you are using the Debugger with DBMS_OUTPUT; see the DBMS Output option in the later "Debugger" section.

Before you execute code that generates output from Oracle's DBMS_OUTPUT package, you need to open the Toad DBMS Output window and enable polling for output from this package. From the Toad Standard toolbar, click on the "Open a new DBMS Output window" button.

Once the window is displayed, verify that the settings are appropriate for what you're planning to do. (The first button on the DBMS Output window toolbar toggles output polling on and off.) Then verify that you have set the DBMS Output buffer to an appropriate size. When Toad encounters a call to DBMS_OUTPUT during stored program execution, that output will be directed to this active window.

You may find it useful to set **Window → Tile Horizontal** to allow you to view both the Procedure Editor and the DBMS Output window at the same time.

TIP

A similar DBMS Output window is available as one of the tabs in the Results panel of the SQL Editor. However, if you open multiple DBMS Output windows, only one will poll for, and subsequently display, output returned by calls to DBMS_OUTPUT.

Find closing block

The **Right Mouse → Find Closing Block** function locates the closing block for a highlighted BEGIN (Toad searches for an END), IF (Toad searches for an ENDIF), or ")" (Toad searches for a ")"). For example, highlight the BEGIN in question, and then select **Right Mouse → Find Closing Block**. The highlight moves to the corresponding END. Note that at this time, this function is unidirectional; it moves from BEGIN to END, not the other way.

Compile

Toad provides several launch points for compiling your program. You can click on the Compile button, the first button on the Procedure Edit toolbar. You can also select **Right Mouse → Compile** or press F9.

If errors occur during compilation, an Errors panel opens at the bottom of the Procedure Editor window displaying the appropriate PLS or ORA error and its description. The line of code where the error was detected is also highlighted in the Code-Editing panel. Compilation stops at the first error that is encountered. Subsequent errors may be discovered after you have corrected the original error and restarted compilation. Sometimes Oracle returns more than one error when you compile a procedure. The Errors panel has arrows on its left side that let you browse through all of the errors returned for the last compile. If you have the Toad for Oracle Professional Edition (see the discussion in the "Additional Toad Modules" section, later in this book), you can also double-click on the error in the panel and bring up the Knowledge Xpert Instant Messages information for that particular error message.

Debugger

The Toad for Oracle Professional Edition has an optional PL/SQL debugging module that provides full debugging capabilities for stored programs (e.g., procedures, functions, triggers, package procedures, and package functions). This module lets you do things such as the following:

- Perform line-by-line debugging and error trapping
- Trace into other PL/SQL objects
- Change the values of variables during runtime
- Set breakpoints and watches; with these, you can monitor specific values inside the procedure, function, or package, as well as the passing/changing of variables passed to the program
- View the results of a returned REF cursor

This section provides a variety of tips for using the Debugger with the Procedure Editor. Much more detailed information is available in the Toad Help files and in the Debugging chapter in the *Toad for Oracle User's Guide*.

TIP

Toad's Debugger utilizes the Oracle Probe API (v2.0 or later). Make sure this software is installed and that Oracle's DBMS_DEBUG package exists under the SYS schema. Each user requires the EXECUTE privilege on DBMS_DEBUG. Oracle Database 10g connections also require the DEBUG CONNECT SESSION privilege.

The Toad Debugger can handle only a single object per tab.

Setting Debugger Options

You can customize the Debugger to suit the way you work. Debugger options are available from **View → Options → Procedure Editor → Debugging**. The following are the options we recommend you consider adopting:

Save proc parameters between sessions

Causes parameters used during execution to be saved between sessions. The parameters are stored in your local *ToadParams.ini* file for reuse the next time you execute the same stored program.

Transaction Control

Provides Commit, Rollback, and Prompt choices. Selecting Commit or Rollback appends an Oracle COMMIT or ROLLBACK statement to the anonymous block created by the Toad Debugger for executing stored programs (see the later section "Setting Parameters" for more details). If you select Prompt (the default), Toad will ask if you want to "Commit changes to debug session?" each time you finish a debug session.

Default to "Compile with Debug"

If this option is checked (the default is unchecked), the "Toggle compiling with Debug" button on the Toad Standard toolbar will be in the on position when each Procedure Editor session begins.

Show executable line indicators in gutter

Causes lines in your code that are eligible for breakpoints to be highlighted with a blue dot in the gutter for that line.

Debugger Menus and Toolbar

You can access Debugger functions from the Toad Debug menu (available from the Toad Menu toolbar and shown in Figure 14), the Debugger toolbar, or the **Procedure Editor → Right Mouse → Debug** menu.

The options are slightly different in each case. The Toad Debug menu (shown here) provides several additional execution options; you can select the "Run to Cursor" function or the "Attach External Session" function, or use the controls for breakpoints and watches.

```
Debug  Window  Help
 ⚡  Run                        F11
 🗒  Run to Cursor              F12
 ⬚  Step Over            Shift+F8
 ⬚  Trace Into           Shift+F7
 ⬚  Trace Out            Shift+F10
 ⬚  Halt Execution
 ⬚  Set Breakpoint       Shift+F5
 ⬚  Add Watch at Cursor  Ctrl+F5
 ⬚  Attach External Session

     Evaluate/Modify      Ctrl+Alt+E

 ⬚  Breakpoints          Ctrl+Alt+B
 ⬚  Call Stack           Ctrl+Alt+S
 ⬚  Watches              Ctrl+Alt+W
 ⬚  DBMS Output          Ctrl+Alt+D
```

Figure 14. Toad Debug menu

The Debugger toolbar (shown in Figure 15) has one option
not available from the Debug menu: the button on the far
right, "Compile dependent objects with Debug". Otherwise,
the icons match the functions on the Debug menu.

Figure 15. Toad Debugger toolbar

The **Procedure Editor → Right Mouse → Debug** menu
(shown in Figure 16) is an abbreviated but handy version of
the main Debug menu and the Debugger toolbar.

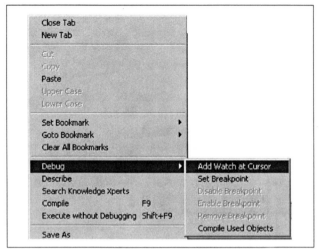

Figure 16. Procedure Editor right mouse Debug menu

Output Panel

The Debugger has a dockable window that can be attached to the Procedure Editor desktop. The Debugger has six tabs, described in the following sections: Breakpoints, Watches, DBMS Output, Call Stack, REF CURSOR Results, and CodeXpert. As usual in Toad, the tabs have unique interior toolbars and right mouse menus.

The REF CURSOR Results tab lies on the Output panel alongside the Debugger display tabs. Note that the REF CURSOR Results tab does not require the Toad for Oracle Professional Edition or the Debugger in order to function.

The CodeXpert tab also lies on the Output panel. Like the Debugger, CodeXpert is part of the Professional Edition. See the later "Using CodeXpert" section for more information.

Breakpoints tab

If you have set a breakpoint on a line, stored program execution will stop before the code on that line is executed. There are several different ways to set and display breakpoints. You can:

- Set a breakpoint by positioning the cursor on the appropriate line of code and clicking F5.
- Set a breakpoint menu by clicking in the editor's gutter to the left of the appropriate line of code.
- Set breakpoints from either of the Debug menus.
- Set conditional breakpoints from **Right Mouse → Edit breakpoint** in the Breakpoint tab. With a conditional breakpoint, execution stops only when a defined condition is met.
- Display breakpoints from the **Debugger → Breakpoints** tab. This tab has an interior toolbar and a right mouse menu with additional breakpoint options.

Note that breakpoints will be honored only at lines that are deemed "executable" by the Oracle Probe API.

Watches tab

If you place a watch on a variable, you can display and evaluate its value during stored program execution. To set a watch, position the cursor on the variable and set the watch from the Debug menu, the Debugger toolbar, or the **Procedure Editor → Right Mouse → Debug** menu. Alternately, position the cursor on the appropriate line of code and press CTRL- F5.

Watches are displayed in the **Debugger → Watches** tab. The tab has an interior toolbar and a right mouse menu that provide additional watch options.

Once you have set a watch, you should review the Watch Properties regularly from the Watches tab by selecting **Right**

Mouse → Edit Watches. The Watch Properties dialog provides an additional option, *Break on a Value Change*, which lets the Debugger use breakpoints more effectively.

Watch variables can be either simple (i.e., scalar) variables or records. When a record is watched, the hover-over will show the values for all of its component variables. When placed in the watch window, records display as a tree of values, with one tree node for each component variable.

In addition to setting a watch to view the value of a variable, you can also hover your mouse cursor over the variable during runtime. Its value will appear in a hover hint box.

DBMS Output tab

Any output generated by calls to the DBMS_OUTPUT package (discussed in the earlier "Procedure Editor" section) during a debugging session is displayed in the **Debugger → DBMS Output** tab. Output is released from the DBMS_OUTPUT buffer after execution has been halted or completed. In nested procedure calls, all procedures must run to completion before any DBMS_OUTPUT results are displayed.

Call Stack tab

The Call Stack window displays the chain of procedures and functions as they are called. The line number references the code line number in the Procedure Editor window. The Call Stack window is active only during execution.

REF CURSOR Results tab

When a debug or execution session terminates, this window displays each table that was created for REF CURSORS via the *Create and write to table* option described in the next section, "Setting Parameters."

Setting Parameters

Before you begin a debugging session, you will need to consider setting values for IN and IN/OUT parameters. You can
set values from **Debug → Set parameters** or by selecting the
"Set Parameters" button on the Debugger toolbar.

The Set Parameters dialog displays the parameter name,
datatype, and IN/OUT mode. Toad now builds an anonymous block to execute the stored program. The block displays in the lower half of the Set Parameters window. As you
enter values, the anonymous block is updated. Alternately,
you can directly edit the generated anonymous block.

Toad assigns NULL values to any IN/OUT parameters whose
values you do not specify.

TIP

When you make changes to the anonymous block, the
"Rebuild Code" button at the bottom of the window becomes active. Use Rebuild Code to resynchronize the
anonymous block with the values entered in the grid.

If your stored PL/SQL object returns a REF CURSOR, you
can select the "Output Options" setting to determine how
the results will be displayed—either via DBMS_OUTPUT or
in a table in the REF CURSOR Results tab.

Just-in-Time Debugging

When performing normal debugging, Toad does two things:
in the first Oracle session it starts an execution of the procedure it is about to debug, and in the second session it traps
the first session into a debugger. Just-in-Time Debugging
allows you to debug PL/SQL code that is written and run
from any client/server application, including Visual Basic,
Delphi, PowerBuilder, Developer/2000, etc. The external
application does not need to exist on the same machine.

This feature is extremely useful when the client/server application calls a stored program with complex parameters, such as cursors, that are not easily simulated from Toad. Rather than trying to simulate the complex environment within Toad, you can simply connect to the external application and then debug the code in its native environment.

To debug package body code that gets executed from a calling program, first compile the package with DEBUG information. Then set a breakpoint within the code, execute the anonymous block from a separate program/session, and finally select the "Attach the External Session" function from the Procedure Editor.

Executing a Stored Program from the Debugger

You can run a stored program by selecting **Debug → Run**, by pressing F11, or by clicking the "Run the current procedure with Debug Info" button on the Debug toolbar. (This button is the same lightning bolt displayed on the **Schema Browser → Procs** toolbar.)

There are additional execution options—for executing the code one line at a time, for stepping over or tracing into procedure or function calls, and for tracing out of a called procedure to return to the caller—on both the Toad Debug menu and the Debugger toolbar.

Executing a Stored Program Without Debugging

Toad allows you to execute a stored program without running it through the Debugger. Select **Procedure Editor → Right Mouse → Execute Without Debugging**. The Execute Without Debugging function opens the Set Parameters dialog and creates the necessary anonymous block (described in the earler section "Setting Parameters").

After Debugging

When you complete a debugging session, there is one final step you need to perform in order to clean up the Debugger's symbol table. Toggle off the "Toggle compiling with debug" button and compile your stored program once more. It will now recompile without the debug symbol tables. This is especially important on production systems as the debug symbols can adversely affect your code's performance.

Code Profiling

Code Profiling is an extremely powerful tool that can be used by developers to identify bottlenecks and code execution problems. Toad uses the Oracle Probe Profiler API to collect performance data on PL/SQL applications. This feature is included in the Toad for Oracle Standard Edition. To use this feature, you must first verify that you have the DBMS_PROFILER package (created by Oracle's *PROFLOAD.sql* script). Then use **Tools → ServerSide Object Wizard** to create Toad's Profiler tables.

Toggle **Database → PL/SQL Profiling** on and then execute your stored program. The Profiler prompts you to name each run (execution). As each run completes, the Profiler Analysis window displays performance data for each line of code. Because this information is stored in database tables, you will be able to run ad hoc queries and customize your own reports. The reports will be viewable from the menu (shown in Figure 17) invoked from **Database → Profiler Analysis**.

Using CodeXpert

CodeXpert is a utility accessible to editors in the Toad for Oracle Professional Edition. This utility provides automatic code reviews for code efficiency, correctness, maintainability, readability, and best practices. CodeXpert can be launched from the CodeXpert tab (see Figure 18) in the Procedure Editor or the SQL Editor.

Figure 17. PL/SQL Profiling and Profiler Analysis options

Figure 18. CodeXpert tab

When run from the Procedure Editor, CodeXpert's entire rulesets are available to validate against PL/SQL, SQL, and SQL*Plus code. When run from the SQL Editor, only the SQL and SQL*Plus rules are tested.

CodeXpert is composed of four components: the Results Tree, the Summary Report, the CRUD Matrix, and the Metrics Report, described in the following sections.

Results tree tab

CodeXpert's Results tree tab allows you to navigate the flagged rules per statement in the code. By default, all rules are listed by Objective (shown in Figure 19) and then by Severity. This ordering can be changed by selecting a different ruleset filter on the CodeXpert status bar and then rerunning the analysis. Clicking on any rule violation will highlight that line of code in the editor window. Toad recognizes that some rules are subjective and that you may not agree with the advice that is being given. You can selectively override any rule or individual occurrence of a rule by right-clicking on it and selecting the *Ignore* option.

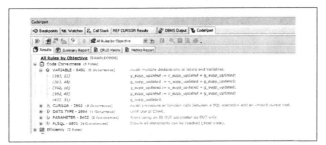

Figure 19. CodeXpert Results Tree

In addition to the flagged rules, the Results tree tab provides access to an analysis of the complexity and soundness of your code (Complexity Metrics) and to a statistical analysis of the code for such items as cursor usage, exception handling, and flow control (Properties).

Summary Report tab

The Summary Report tab provides a visual overview of analysis results using pie and bar charts. Additional insights about the meaning of any Objective or Severity can be displayed by hovering the cursor over its name.

CRUD Matrix tab

The CRUD Matrix tab provides a tabular representation of the data access for the analyzed SQL or PL/SQL code. The name CRUD is derived from the list of possible tabular DML actions: Create (i.e., INSERT), Retrieve (i.e., SELECT), Update, and Delete.

Metrics Report tab

The Metrics Report tab gives insights into the complexity of your code (using the Halstead Volume computational complexity algorithm), the soundness or confidence level of your code (using McCabe's Cyclomatic Complexity method), and a quantitative analysis of the code's maintainability. These metrics are also available from the Results Tree tab.

CodeXpert toolbar

CodeXpert analyses may be activated and configured using its toolbar buttons. These consist of:

Run
> Runs a new analysis for the current edit window contents.

Include Ruleset
> Enables/disables this option. When enabled, the selected ruleset will be run against the editor contents. When disabled, no rules will be tested; only a SQL scan will be done.

Scan SQL Statements
> Enables/disables this option. When enabled, all SQL contained in the edit window will be checked for ways to optimize it. When disabled, no optimization checks will be performed.

Configure Optimization
> Allows the user to define both that which should be scanned and rules for SQL classification (simple, complex, and problematic).

Find in Tree
> Provides a means to do a quick lookup of a rule number rather than manually scanning through the tree entries.

Show Tip
> Enables when a rule node is selected in the tree. Clicking this button will display additional insights on the rule violation.

Rule Set
> Provides a dropdown list of CodeXpert's supplied rule filters.

Configure Rulesets
> Provides a means to create a user-defined filter and view details on the supplied ruleset filters.

Legend
> Displays meanings of the various icons used in CodeXpert.

Zoom
> Opens the Summary Report in a separate window that can be expanded to full screen for easier reading.

Save
> Provides a means to save the Summary, CRUD, or Metrics Report.

Print Preview
> Allows the user to view how the printed report will look.

Print
> Prints the Summary, CRUD, or Metrics Report (depending on which is active).

Database Administration

Toad provides a powerful but easy-to-use interface for managing the many ongoing tasks associated with Oracle database administration. You can use Toad in conjunction with routine Oracle maintenance activities (e.g., monitoring user activity, space usage, etc.), as well as with less routine activities like creating new databases.

You can access database administration functions from various locations in Toad, including the Schema Browser window and the Create, Database, Tools, and View menus. A number of these functions are located on Toad's DBA menu, and several require that the add-on DBA Module be licensed. In the following sections, we'll label each entry according to the function's location in Toad.

User management and other aspects of user administration are also key parts of overall database administration; we address these topics in the later section "User Administration."

Using the DBA Module

The DBA Module is an optional, add-on configuration of Toad with features designed especially for use by the Oracle DBA.

Additional functionality

The DBA Module adds extended functionality to Toad's Schema Browser, Create menu, and DBA menu as follows:

Schema Browser
> Displays additional tabs for such objects as directories, libraries, policies, profiles, rollback segments, roles, snapshots, snapshot logs, and tablespaces (see the earlier "Schema Browser" section for a full list)

Create menu
> Provides the ability to create the items added to the Schema Browser

DBA menu
> Displays the following additional screens:
>> Audit Objects
>> Audit SQL/SYS Privs
>> Compare Databases
>> Compare Schemas
>> Control Files

Database Browser
Database Health Check
Database Monitor
Database Probe
Data Pump Import/Export Wizards
Data Pump Job Manager
Generate Database Script
Generate Schema Script
Index Monitoring
Instance Manager
Log Miner
Log Switch Frequency Map
New (Create) Database Wizard
Pinned Code
Redo Log Manager
Resource Plan Scheduling
SQL Loader Interface
Tablespaces Map
Top Session Finder
UNDO Advisor
Unix Job Scheduler
Unix Kernel Parms
Unix Monitor
Windows Registry Parms

Knowledge Xpert for Oracle Administration

The DBA Module includes a component known as the
Knowledge Xpert for Oracle Administration. The Knowledge Xpert is a comprehensive Windows-based technical
resource that fully anticipates the daily responsibilities of
DBAs. Thousands of topics provide the insights, database
analysis information, and working examples DBAs need to
troubleshoot problems and apply solutions.

The Knowledge Xpert is accessible from Toad via the Standard toolbar. When Toad encounters an Oracle error message, you can double-click on the message number; the
Knowledge Xpert automatically opens to that topic.

Using the Database Browser

Selecting **Database** → **Database Browser** invokes the Database Browser, which displays information across multiple databases and/or servers; you can select multiple databases or servers, view a variety of summary information for them, perform Pings and TNSPings on them, and open common Toad windows for them.

The Database Browser reads your *TNSNAMES.ora* file and builds a list of servers and databases. You can then use Toad's connect screen to open a session against the database you want to browse. You can configure instances to autoconnect once the Database Browser window is opened. One of the convenient features of this window is its ability to collect statistics against *all* of the instances running on a single server and display them on a single screen. For example, the browser could monitor the rollback segments across multiple instances on a single Unix server.

When the Database Browser is able to roll up information across instances, you will be presented with a multirecord grid view. Otherwise, you'll see a single-record view that you can use to peruse information, one instance at a time.

The Database Browser can launch the Database Health Check, the Database Monitor, the Session Browser, and several other screens against a connected instance to get more in-depth information for the database you are browsing.

The Database Browser has full support for running against Real Application Clusters (RAC) instances. When RAC is detected, this screen's information will be gathered from the appropriate GV$ tables. You will simply note the addition of an extra column in grid outputs for the instance ID. Moreover, this screen is aware of the current connection's instance versus the instance of a requested operation, and will autoconnect to the proper instance, perform the task and then disconnect—all without requiring you to do anything.

Modifying Oracle Parameters

There is an Oracle Parameters tab within the Database Browser screen, but the Oracle Parameters screen provides much more powerful capabilities, allowing you to view Oracle's *INIT.ora* file from Toad. Selecting **DBA → Oracle Parameters** opens a window that displays your *INIT.ora* parameters in a grid format with the following column headings:

Option
Displays the parameter name.

Settings
Shows the current value specified for that parameter.

Default
Indicates whether the current parameter value is set to the default value.

Description
Provides a brief description of the parameter's function.

Session Modifiable, System Modifiable
Both columns display "Yes" or "No", indicating the parameter's modifiable status.

You can search, print, or save an instance's list of initialization parameters by using the Oracle Parameters window's toolbar.

If you have the DBA Module installed, you can modify many of the Oracle initialization parameters in the *INIT.ora* file from within the grid. (Users who do not have the DBA Module are limited to viewing the *INIT.ora* file via Toad.)

To modify a parameter, double-click on the desired parameter in the displayed grid or press the Edit button with the appropriate parameter selected. If the parameter you want to change is either system-modifiable or session-modifiable, a popup dialog box opens. Enter the new value into that box.

TIP

If a parameter is both session-modifiable *and* system-modifiable, Toad will modify it at the system level. Be aware that session-level parameters are modified for the current session only. Changed system-modifiable parameters do not persist after a database reboot.

The Oracle Parameters screen has full support for running against RAC instances. All relevant information for the grid output will be gathered from the appropriate GV$ tables. You will simply note the addition of an extra column in grid outputs for the instance ID. Parameters are sorted by default according to parameter name and then instance ID, so you will see groupings of each parameter's settings across RAC instances together. You can change the screen style to a separate tab per RAC instance simply by checking the checkbox in the screen's toolbar (which displays only when RAC is detected).

Managing Sessions

Toad has two screens for viewing information for a session or group of sessions:

DBA → Top Session Finder
Allows you to assign weights to hundreds of different session statistics. The window will then apply these to identify the sessions that meet these criteria.

DBA → Session Browser
Allows you to easily view and work with sessions—for example, you can kill a session, start/stop a trace, view session locks, view transaction information, and much more.

Top Session Finder

This window identifies sessions in the database that are consuming the most resources. Oracle tracks hundreds of statistics for each session in the database, and the Top Session Finder allows you to easily sort the sessions by their usage of any combination of parameters.

You can operate the Top Session Finder in either of these modes:

Single parameter select mode
Lists sessions in order of resource usage. You click the name of the resource of interest.

Multiple parameter select mode
Lets you assign weights to two or more parameters; the sessions are sorted by the weighted sum of the statistics.

The Top Session Finder has full support for running against RAC instances. When RAC is detected, this screen's information will be gathered from the appropriate GV$ tables. You will simply note the addition of an extra column in grid outputs for the instance ID. Moreover, this screen is aware of the current connection's instance versus the instance of a requested operation, and will autoconnect to the proper instance, perform the task, and then disconnect—all without requiring you to do anything.

Session Browser

The Session Browser was introduced in Toad Version 7.6, and completely replaced the Kill/Trace screen in Version 8.0. The Session Browser displays parallel slave information, allows multiselect, shows more detailed locks information, collects and displays session information across RAC instances, and lets you create your own filters for use in the window.

Here are some hints to make the Session Browser look similar to the previous Kill/Trace screen:

- Press "Flip form layout" to make the tabs appear at the bottom of the window instead of on the righthand side.
- Under the "Group by" button, select "none" to eliminate the treeview.
- Press "Visible columns" to get a list of the columns that you can display in the list of sessions.

The Session Browser shares some behavior found in Toad's Database Browser screen. Sessions can be multiselected; in this case, the browser will collect information across the sessions and display it all on one screen.

The Session Browser has full support for running against RAC instances. When RAC is detected, this screen's information will be gathered from the appropriate GV$ tables. You will simply note the addition of an extra column in grid outputs for the instance ID. Moreover, this screen is aware of the current connection's instance versus the instance of a requested operation, and will autoconnect to the proper instance, perform the task, and then disconnect—all without requiring you to do anything.

Creating and Altering Objects

Toad's Create and Alter dialogs help DBAs to manage their database objects. For example, you can quickly create a roll-back segment from Toad's Create menu or from the Rollback Segments Schema Browser tab. This section describes objects you can manage if the DBA Module is present.

Create new objects

You can use the Create dialog available from the Create menu to quickly create a database object without having to worry about syntax or typographical errors.

The Create/Alter dialogs are fully fleshed out to display all of the DDL options supported by Oracle (options not available and activated are greyed out). The dialogs are smart enough to detect the Oracle version you are connected to and to enable/disable the appropriate options. Figure 20 shows a portion of the menu invoked by selecting **DBA → Create**.

If you have a role in one instance, you can use the handy Schema Browser function, Create Like, to create the same role in another instance. You can even modify the script that will be executed if you want to tweak the role you are moving.

Alter existing objects

You can use Toad's Alter dialogs to make a change to an existing object. You can access these directly from the Schema Browser or, if you are querying an object in an editor and you need to modify or examine the object(s) at hand, you can simply place your cursor on the object and press F4. This will bring up the Describe popup window. From here you can examine the object, view/alter the data, or alter the object.

Managing Tablespaces

Three primary windows are available in Toad for managing tablespaces:

Figure 20. A portion of the Toad Create menu

DBA → Segment Management → Tablespaces

Allows you to manage files, monitor free space, view segments, display fragmentation, and access Space Manager to track and forecast database usage over time.

DBA → Segment Management → Tablespace Map

Provides a graphical view of how space is allocated to objects in the tablespaces in your database. This lets you view segment fragmentation by tablespace.

Schema Browser → Tablespaces Tab

Allows you to view your tablespaces, create new ones, alter existing ones, generate DDL scripts, and so on.

Display tablespace statistics

To obtain a detailed, multitabbed view of all of your tablespace statistics, select either **Schema Browser** → **Tablespaces** or **DBA** → **Tablespaces**. Both approaches let you create or modify tablespaces and create or modify datafiles, and both provide Datafiles, Free Space, Objects, and Fragmentation tabs. But there are some differences between the two approaches:

- **Schema Browser** → **Tablespaces** details one tablespace at a time, while **DBA** → **Tablespaces** generally displays information on all tablespaces in a grid. This is the major difference between the two approaches.

- Only **Schema Browser** → **Tablespaces** has an Extents tab and a Properties tab.

- Only **DBA** → **Tablespaces** has a Space History tab and an IO History tab.

Both approaches provide the following information in tabs:

Datafiles
> Displays the tablespaces and their associated datafiles with a complete path description, online/offline status, and extent information. You can sort the information in the displayed grid by clicking on any column header.

Free Space (in KB)
> Displays the number of blocks and the minimum, average, maximum, and total amount of free space for each tablespace in grid format. As with the Datafiles display, you can sort the data in the grid by clicking on any column header.

Objects
> Is populated after you select a tablespace name from the dropdown menu. Details on all the objects, including owner, name, and object type, are displayed in a sortable grid format along with each object's extent information, which includes the extent, next extent, number of extents, maximum extents, and size of the extents in

bytes and MB. (The use of **DBA** → **Extents**, which provides extent information by selected schema rather than by tablespace, is discussed later in "Checking Extents.")

Fragmentation

Displays fragmentation information by tablespace. The grid includes columns showing total blocks, empty blocks, number of fragments (pieces), size of fragments, and number of usable fragments.

Display tablespace map

DBA → **Segment Management** → **Tablespace Map** displays a tablespace map. As you mouse over cells in the map for a given tablespace, Toad displays the segments that consume data blocks represented by that cell. However, if the tablespace is large, that cell might represent hundreds of actual data blocks, and in this case they may not overlap at all. Keep in mind that red cells really represent segments that consume a high percentage of blocks for their overall size, and may be candidates for object rebuilds.

TIP

The tablespace map uses a simplified fragmentation formula. Key elements of the formula are:

- The sum of the blocks for that segment
- The largest block in that segment

In Oracle, there are many different kinds of fragmentation—and just as many opinions on which ones really matter and/or how they should be calculated. One type of fragmentation attempts to measure the relative fragmentation of a segment within a tablespace. Although this type of fragmentation has many names, it is most often called *internal fragmentation* because it measures the fragmentation of the object within the tablespace. (Toad uses this type of measurement.) These days, with locally managed tablespaces, uniform extents, and no disadvantage to zillions of extents (as there were in the past), this might not be as relevant a measurement as it once was.

Checking Extents

You can identify space-bound objects by checking their defined Next Extent values. Selecting **DBA** → **Extents** opens the View Extents window, which displays the datafile extents information by selected schema.

The default display is All Objects, but you can restrict the selection by choosing only to display tables, indexes, rollback segments, or clusters. After choosing All Objects or the selected object types, select the owner from the dropdown list. Once you click on the Go button on the toolbar, Toad displays the following columns in the grid: Object Name, Type, Tablespace, Total Size (in KB), Initial Extent, Next Extent, (existing) Extents, and Max Extents. Click on the column header to apply an ascending or descending sort.

We recommend that you print and review this extent information often to keep up with growth trends in your database.

TIP

DBA → **Extents** requires access to DBA views in order to select owners from the dropdown list. Otherwise, Toad uses SYS.USER_EXTENTS to populate the View Extents window with the logged-in user's information.

Using Oracle's Import/Export Tools

Toad has two sets of tools for accommodating Oracle imports and exports:

DBA → **Data Import/Export** → **Export/Import Utility Wizards**
  Provides a wizard interface to Oracle's IMP and EXP programs.

DBA → **Data Import/Export** → **Export/Data Pump Export/ Import Utility Wizards**
  Provides a wizard interface to Oracle Database 10*g*'s Data Pump, which is a replacement for the IMP and EXP utilities.

Both sets of wizards allow you to easily create a parameter file for an Export, Import, or Data Pump session. The wizards also allow you to use the Windows Scheduler to schedule an Import or Export session at a later time. The Data Pump interface also comes with a Data Pump Job Manager with which you can manage your Data Pump jobs.

Export File Browser

The Export File Browser is available for users with the DBA Module or the Toad for Oracle Professional Edition. It can be found under the DBA menu within the "Data Export and Import" submenu.

The Export File Browser window lets you browse Oracle Export files. You can see what objects are in them or get DDL for one or multiple objects (or for a whole schema). You can also look at the data of any table (or partition of a table) in a grid, and use Toad's "Grid...Save as" or "Grid... Print" functions.

Using Toad's Export File Browser, you can browse easily through export files and view such file information as schemas, DDL, data, functions/packages/procedures/triggers, object type bodies, tuning and configuration, and refresh groups.

Using Other Toad Import/Export Utilities

Toad provides a number of Oracle Import/Export options. These can be found in the appropriate Schema Browser tabs, Grid menu, SQL Editor Data tab right mouse menu, Database menu, and DBA menu. Many of the options on the Database menu are also available in the Schema Browser. Note, however, that the export options vary; the Schema Browser is single-object-oriented, while the **Database** → **Export** functions can handle multiple objects.

Database → Export → Export Table Scripts

Use this function to export the table scripts for a designated schema/owner. When you select the schema/owner name from the dropdown menu at the top of the screen, the table names for that schema/owner display in a long list; you can change that list to a columnar display by using the arrows at the lower left of the screen. You can select a single table, multiple tables, or all tables (via the Select All button at the bottom of the screen).

Database → Export → Grants

The Grants function follows a similar but simpler format for exporting the grants on all objects for a specified user. You can limit the export to include only grants issued by the selected schema. You can also direct the output to the clipboard or to a single designated file.

Database → Export → Table Data

The Table Data function exports the data for a single table or for all tables for a designated schema/owner. From the Options tab you can exclude null columns, include the schema/owner name in the INSERT statements, and direct the output to a single file or to a separate file for each table. As with the **Database → Export → Export Table Scripts** option, when separate files are created, Toad uses the table name as the file name.

Schema Browser → Tables → Export Data

The Export Data function available from the Schema Browser window is slightly different from **Database → Export → Data Export**. In the Schema Browser you are limited to exporting data from one table at a time. Right-click on a table name in the Tables tab and select Export Data. The Schema Browser export has options to export to a clipboard and an optional WHERE clause for filtering the data. You can also select particular columns to export, and choose how often to insert COMMIT statements.

Database → Export → Source Code

The Source Code function exports the code for your selected schema's stored programs as SQL script files. The Source Code Export window includes selection options for choosing all the objects for a designated schema. You can also limit the selection to source code for all programs of a type—for example, all packages, all procedures, all functions, all triggers, or all views. You also can select from the options *Create one file for all objects* or *Each object to a separate file*.

If you choose *Group objects in the following files*, Toad will create separate files for all procedures, all triggers, and so on.

If you select a single object type, an additional tab opens, allowing you to choose specific objects to include or exclude from the export. If you select all objects, tabs for selecting and unselecting individual stored programs do not display.

Database → Export → Table as Flat File

This function creates a *flat file*. By definition, a flat file is a file that does not contain TAB characters or comma characters (,) between values. A flat file also requires the creation of a companion Specifications file, which defines the table name, the table owner, how many lines in the output file will be covered by a single record of data, the columns of data, the line on which they will appear, the starting column, and the length of each column of data. This function handles all the details of creating both the flat file and the Specifications file.

Comparing Schemas and Databases

Use **DBA → Compare Schemas** to ensure that schemas look identical across environments (especially across development, test, and production environments). Compare Schemas generates a detailed comparison report. This function lets you create a synchronization script to bring the schemas into uniformity. It will work for schemas on the same instance or on different instances. Note that this function does not examine data.

TIP

If you want to compare the data between two tables or views, then consider using Toad's Compare Data screen found under the Tools menu.

Compare Schemas does not provide details on database-level objects such as users and tablespaces, but you can use **DBA → Compare Databases** for this purpose. The Compare Databases window lets you compare two databases and tells you what has changed from the original reference source to the comparison source.

Performing SGA Trace Optimization

You can use **Tools → SGA Trace Optimization** to view information about SQL statements that have been executed and the resources used by those statements. While Auto Trace and TKPROF information are specific to a single statement, SGA Trace Optimization displays statistics from multiple SQL statements currently present in Oracle's System Global Area (SGA).

Go to **Tools → SGA Trace Optimization** to open the SGA Trace window. You can set several options from this screen in order to search for SQL statements. The default settings are for "ALL Statements" for "ALL Users", but you can click on the corresponding dropdown list and choose another option to change these choices. You can limit the selection to a single statement type (e.g., SELECT statements, UPDATE statements, anonymous PL/SQL, etc.) or to a specific user. You can also enter a text string in the SQL Search Text box to limit the rows returned to statements containing that text string.

Click on the "Refresh the List of Statements" button to retrieve the most resource-intensive SQL from the SGA. Clicking this returns all of the queries that match your criteria. The screen is divided into two parts:

Top half
> Displays the query results, which show the query that was executed and the associated resources used (memory, disk reads, loads, etc.)

Bottom half
> Displays the full SQL statement, execution statistics from the Oracle shared pool, and the Explain Plan for the query

When necessary, you can pass a SQL statement into the SQL Editor from the SGA Trace window. Highlight the desired statement, then click on the "Load selected statement in a SQL Editor" button on the SGA Trace toolbar.

This toolbar also contains a button to "Flush the SGA". The Oracle privileges of the logged-in user dictate your ability to use this function.

TIP

Tools → **SGA Trace Optimization** requires access to a number of Oracle V$ objects. For a current listing of the Oracle access required to utilize this feature, go to **Help** → **Contents**. From the Table of Contents, select **Toad Basics** → **V$ Tables Required**.

The SGA Trace Optimization screen has full support for running against RAC instances. When RAC is detected, this screen's information will be gathered from the appropriate GV$ tables. You will simply note the addition of an extra column in grid outputs for the instance ID. Moreover, this screen is aware of the current connection's instance versus the instance of a requested operation, and will autoconnect to the proper instance, perform the task, and then disconnect—all without requiring you to do anything.

Using the HTML Schema Doc Generator

Toad gives you various tools that allow you to document many areas of your database. The most powerful one is probably the **Tools → HTML Schema Doc Generator**. This window lets you select one or more schemas from the left panel and create HTML documentation describing those schemas. Hyperlinks throughout the final HTML document let you jump between sections of the documentation.

This is a great tool for development teams working on a dynamic project that requires frequent database changes. The DBA can schedule this window to run from Toad automatically by taking advantage of Toad's command-line run support. In the HTML Schema Doc Generator setup screen, save the options layout to a file. Then, using your OS Scheduler, have this command run at the desired interval:

```
c:\Toad\Toad.exe Connect=system/manager@mydb GENHTML=
    c:\thisfile.txt
```

The HTML formatting options allow you to use your own Cascading Style Sheets (CSS) to dictate how the HTML appears. If you are not comfortable with CSS, you can manually set the fonts, background images, colors, and so on.

User Administration

Toad provides a number of tools that help the DBA perform user administration tasks. These tools allow you to create users, roles, profiles, storage, grants, and quotas. You can also use Toad to monitor users and users' objects and tablespaces. Like the previous section, "Database Administration," this section is aimed at DBAs.

You can select any of the following:

Schema Browser → Users

Allows you to review and modify a user's assigned roles, privileges, and storage. Users can also be locked/unlocked, modified, and cloned from the Users tab toolbar and the right mouse menu.

Schema Browser → Roles

Allows you to create, alter, and drop roles, configure grantees for roles, and create scripts to re-create your roles in other schemas.

Schema Browser → Resource Groups & Resource Plans

Allows you to define resource plans and groups assigned to users and roles. This functionality requires the optional DBA Module.

Schema Browser → Policies & Policy Groups

Allows you to administer your policies and policy groups. This functionality requires the optional DBA Module and at least an Oracle8*i* Database connection.

Schema Browser → Sys Privs

Allows you to administer all of your system privileges. In this way you can see who has been granted SYS privileges in your database.

DBA → Auditing → Audit SQL/SYS Privs

Allows you to set the audit monitoring options for SQL statement objects, reserved words, and system privileges in the database. This functionality requires the optional DBA Module.

DBA → Auditing → Audit Objects

Allows you to set the audit monitoring options for your database objects. This functionality requires the optional DBA Module.

Managing Users

Managing all of the users across multiple databases can be a daunting task, even for a skilled DBA. Toad offers several tools to help make your job more manageable. The Users tab available from the Schema Browser provides a centralized place to perform all of your user administration tasks.

Create User and Alter User

As with Toad's other Create and Alter Object dialogs, the Create User and Alter User functions allow you to set up a user account in one fell swoop. Not only can you set up the desired CREATE USER statement, you can also configure the user account's system privileges, object grants, quotas, and resource groups. When you do, Toad will create a script and send it to Toad's Script Engine to create the user account.

On the Tablespace tab, Toad has an option to set your selections for the user's default and temporary tablespaces as defaults for all future Create User sessions in Toad for the current database. Enable the *Set Tablespace names as defaults for all User Creates* option to have Toad remember your selections.

Perhaps you have an existing user account that you wish to use as a model for creating a new account. In the Schema Browser, right-click on the existing user on the lefthand side of the Schema Browser and select Clone/Copy. Toad will allow you to specify the name of the new account and the authentication method and/or password. The current user's role grants, system privileges, and so on are used to create the new user.

Compare users

The amount of information contained in a user's profile can be overwhelming. Toad requires nine tabs in the Schema Browser Detail tab just to display all of the information for a single user. When you need to compare two user accounts, you can simplify the task by using the Schema Browser right-click "Compare with another user" function.

Toad will analyze the differences between the two accounts and present an easy-to-read accounting report. If you have the DBA Module, you can take the migration script generated by Toad and use it to synch the two users.

Toad Security

Toad displays all of the Oracle commands available to a user based on that user's Oracle privileges. However, Toad may present some functionality to a user that you, as the DBA, want to prevent that user from exercising. One example is the Truncate Table functionality in the Schema Browser. While some DBAs prefer to handle database security themselves via their own user and role management, others may want to manually disable Toad functionality for certain users or groups of users.

You can use the Toad Security facility, available from **Tools → Toad Security**, to restrict Toad users from having access to specific Toad features. By default, users are granted access to all features of Toad. With Toad Security, you can restrict individuals or groups of users from accessing particular Toad features, and you can also make Toad read-only for specific individuals or groups of users.

WARNING

Toad Security read-only affects only the Toad for Oracle Standard Edition. If you have the Debugger or the DBA Module, those module components will remain fully accessible.

Managing Roles

Toad makes working with roles in Oracle as painless as possible. You can quickly determine exactly what a role is composed of and who has been granted that role. You can also create a new role or alter an existing one.

Configure Grantees

To see what roles a user has been granted, simply choose that user in the Schema Browser and select the Role Grants tab on the Detail panel. However, if you want to determine who in your database has been granted access to a given role, you must proceed to the Roles tab in the Schema Browser, right-click, and select Configure Grantees. The Configure Grantees screen lets you examine which roles in the database have been granted and defaulted, and which users have been granted admin privileges. You can even "copy" over the details from another role.

This functionality requires the optional DBA Module.

Managing Resource Groups and Resource Plans

If you have the optional DBA Module, Toad will provide tabs in the Schema Browser for managing your database's resource consumer groups and resource plans. By managing resource groups and plans in this way, you will not have to bother remembering the syntax for Oracle's DBMS_RESOURCE_MANAGER package.

With the Alter Resource Plan button you can set degrees of parallelism, execution time, and group switching triggers all in one screen.

With the Resource Groups tab in the Schema Browser, you can quickly determine the grantees of a given resource group and the plans assigned to a group. Each plan also has a status indicator.

While resource consumer groups are being created, they reside in a "pending" area. If errors occur during the process of creating/altering/dropping a resource consumer group, objects may remain in the pending area. Toad will usually clear the pending area when errors occur, but you can use Toad's right-click "Clear pending area" function to clear the pending area manually if necessary.

The Users tab in the Schema Browser also displays the resource groups assigned to the user in the Resource Groups tab located in the Detail panel. You can revoke a switch on the selected resource group for the user.

Managing Policies and Policy Groups

If you have the optional DBA Module, Toad will provide tabs in the Schema Browser for managing your database's policies and policy groups. You can determine if your table has had a policy applied to it by browsing the "Policies" Detail panel tab within the Users tab in the Schema Browser.

Auditing

In 2002 the United States Senate passed the Sarbanes-Oxley Act, legislation sponsored by Banking Committee chairman Paul Sarbanes to tighten regulation of independent auditors and make company officers more accountable for their conduct. Companies must now comply with this legislation and, in some cases, companies may not be allowed to purchase software that does not provide the relevant auditing capabilities.

Oracle has had auditing capabilities for several releases. Toad now has an interface to Oracle's auditing administration and audit trails, which is described in later sections. You can select:

DBA → Auditing → Audit SQL/SYS Privs
Allows you to configure the audit monitoring options for SQL statement objects, reserved words, and system privileges in the database. This functionality requires the optional DBA Module.

Database → Auditing → Audit Objects

Displays a window showing the audit monitoring options for selected database objects. You can enter and modify monitoring levels for each individual object or for groups of objects. This functionality requires the optional DBA Module.

Audit SQL/SYS Privs

This screen has two display views:

Audit Options

Displays all of the SQL statements and SYS Privs statements that may be audited.

Audit Trail

Displays the auditing data recorded.

Before an audit trail can be compiled, auditing must be enabled on the database. Auditing screens also require the AUDIT SYSTEM privilege and the AUDIT ANY system privilege.

Use the Schema dropdown control to determine if the auditing options you enable will be applied to a single schema or to the entire database. Once you have chosen the statement on which you want to enable auditing, double-click on the Value cell in the data grid. This will open the View/Edit Audit Option window.

Once you have configured your auditing options and enabled auditing on your instance, you are ready to view the audit trail. The audit trail can be exported using the **Grid → Save As** function. You may find the XLS Instance (Excel) function the most user-friendly; it exports the entire audit trail to a new Excel spreadsheet, even bringing over the column labels if desired.

Audit objects

This screen allows the DBA to set the auditing options for all of the objects in the database: directories, libraries, object

---

types, procedures/functions/packages, sequences, snapshots/materialized views, tables, and views.

You can select the objects by type, by user, or by a combination of both. Once you have the objects loaded into the grid, you can set the auditing options. You can set these options across objects or pick and choose the options in the grid array for each object. Once you have set your options, use the Apply Changes button to post the audit settings to the database.

To view the audit trail for the objects on which you have enabled auditing, navigate to the particular object in the Schema Browser. The Auditing tab on the Detail panel provides you with two views:

Audit Options
> Allows you to configure the auditing options for the individual object (versus using the Audit Objects screen and loading the object manually)

Audit Trail
> Allows you to access the audit trail for the object selected on the lefthand side of the Schema Browser

Project Manager

Toad's Project Manager (PM), which may be accessed from the Tools menu dropdown, represents a paradigm shift in the development of new windows and functionality in Toad. Instead of providing the user a new GUI interface for an Oracle operation, the PM delivers to the user a centralized screen that allows him to manage his most frequently related objects and database tasks. The window is organized in a tree structure, where every item in the tree is a node that points to a different object (see Figure 21).

For example, most Toad users' day-to-day tasks are not limited to interacting with Oracle objects (e.g., tables, indexes, snapshots, etc.). You also work with files, maintain web pages,

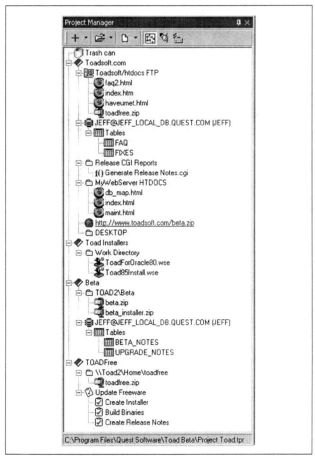

Figure 21. Project Manager display

and so on. The PM provides a centralized area to manage items that are related within a given project, allowing you to:

- Take advantage of integrated operating system operations and Toad file operations (e.g., open, delete, compress, compare, FTP/SFTP, print, etc.)

- Perform full database object operations (F4) (e.g., generate DLL, alter, drop, compare with another object, etc.)
- Administer named SQL collections
- Keep to-do lists
- Manage Windows Scheduler tasks

Creating and Using Projects

The PM opens with a default project loaded. The contents of a Toad project are stored in a project (*.tpr*) file. A project file can actually hold multiple project nodes. Nodes may be of the following types:

File Folder
Represents a folder on a local or network disk.

File
Represents a file on a local or network disk.

FTP Folder
Represents a folder on an FTP server. Contains FTP files.

FTP File
Represents a file on an FTP server.

DB Schema
Represents a connection to a schema on a database. Can contain database objects.

DB Object
Represents an object residing on a database. Must be contained in a DB Schema node.

To Do List
Represents a user-created checklist.

URL
Represents a URL and can act as a shortcut to that web address.

SubProject
May be used to further organize your project nodes.

To add a project child node, select your project and either **Right Mouse → Add** or use the PM toolbar Add Item button. To add a database connection node or database object node, you must first connect to the instance as the user whose privileges you want the PM to use to access the desired instance and objects.

The PM displays available functions via three different interfaces:

- Drag-and-drop
- Double-click
- Popup menus

For example, if you drag an FTP File Folder item on top of a database object, Toad will FTP the file, and do a file compare based on the object's generated DLL. If you double-click on a database object, Toad will do an F4 Describe. And if you **Right Mouse** on a DB schema, you can connect to the specified schema or open a Procedure Editor against it.

Customizing Project Manager's Behavior

The PM's most powerful characteristic is its user configurability. You can set up the PM to load your own particular file associations, program desired popup operations, specify the drag-and-drop operation for each node type, and define what will happen on double-clicks for each PM node type.

To see what the PM can really do, bring up the Options dialog by pushing the Options button on the PM toolbar. The Options interface has six pages of options:

- General
- Associations
- Drag-and-drop operations
- Double-click operations
- Popup menus
- DDL

The drag-and-drop operations, double-click operations, and popup menus pages are where you define what happens for each of those operations. Drag-and-drop and double-click options are presented in a grid. Click on the "Perform this action" column contents to bring up a dropdown selector. The popup menus options page has a tree control where you can check/uncheck the popup you want to appear when you **Right Mouse** on a PM node.

The Associations options page defines all of the file types the PM will be handling and which applications will be available to each. Each defined application is associated with file extensions, a working directory, and command-line parameters.

The DDL options page is used to configure Toad's DDL engine, which determines exactly what DDL clauses will be generated for each database object when comparing objects, for example, or sending an object's DDL to a file or to a Toad editor.

Saving and Sharing Project Files

The PM can load any project (*.tpr*) file. Toad allows you to keep different sets of project files, and a project file can be opened from anywhere on the network.

A project team leader might want to create a project file for all of the project team members to share. Use the Save Project and Open Project buttons on the PM toolbar to manage your PM files.

Project Manager Tips and Tricks

Here are some suggestions for using the Project Manager most effectively.

- Use the PM's full file archiving functionality, which allows you to create and manage your own Zip archives.
- Move files seamlessly between your PC and remote file servers via drag-and-drop FTP.

- Download *www.Toadsoft.com* files (beta, freeware, QSR, Release Notes) via drag-and-drops on URLs.
- Manage any directory on your PC; you will see only the files you want.
- Give your directory logical names (e.g., *ToadTemps* instead of *C:\Program Files\Quest Software\Toad\User Files)*.
- Filter directory contents—for example, create a filter on your workspace to show only your Delphi project files.
- Add an item to your project from the Schema Browser by right-clicking on the object.
- Create a project for each day of the work week to organize your tasks.
- Use the "Toggle reorder mode" button to arrange the node ordering.
- Access Oracle's Export utility by using **Right Mouse** on a file folder item with a *.dat* extension.
- Remove register dumps by using **Right Mouse** on an FTP folder item with a *.trc* extension.
- Use FTP folder right-click operations such as RExec and Telnet.
- Use FTP folder item right-click operations such as Compress and Touch.

Additional Toad Modules

Toad comes in four configurations to match users' different database editing and administration needs:

- Toad for Oracle
- Toad for Oracle Professional Edition
- Toad for Oracle Xpert Edition
- Toad for Oracle Suite

Each is described briefly in the following sections. Consult the Toad Help files or the Quest web site (*http://www.quest.com/toad/index.asp*) for more information.

Toad for Oracle

Toad for Oracle provides the foundation and basic tools Oracle professionals need in order to create and execute queries, as well as build and manage database objects. This edition enables you to plug into Toad's added utilities.

Toad for Oracle Professional Edition

The Professional Edition includes all of the features of Toad for Oracle, but adds several key features (mentioned throughout the book). These include the debugging of stored programs (within the Procedure Editor) and SQL*Plus scripts (within the SQL Editor). Also included are CodeXpert (which analyzes stored procedures against a set of best-practice rules) and Knowledge Xpert for PL/SQL (which provides background information on thousands of topics, including syntax and working PL/SQL examples).

Toad for Oracle Xpert Edition

The Toad for Oracle Xpert Edition includes all of the features of the Toad for Oracle Professional Edition plus a powerful SQL tuning component that simplifies the task of identifying potential performance problems.

Toad for Oracle Suite

The Toad for Oracle Suite includes all of the features and functionality found in the Toad for Oracle Xpert Edition plus a built-in array of tools: the Toad-DBA Module, DataFactory™, Benchmark Factory® for Oracle, and QDesigner™ Physical Architect. This complete development suite provides all the tools necessary to design, develop, test, and manage your database. Note that each of the add-ons described below can also be added to any of the other Toad editions.

Toad-DBA Module

The Toad-DBA Module activates additional menu items in Toad's Create menu, DBA menu, and Schema Browser. It also adds functionality to existing menu items; for example, with the DBA Module installed, the Import/Export Utility wizards include the SQL*Loader interface. Also included with the DBA Module is the Knowledge Xpert for Oracle Administration, which provides answers to daily administration questions with thousands of topics, syntax diagrams, and step-by-step methodologies.

DataFactory™

DataFactory™ is a data generator that allows developers and QA personnel to easily populate test databases with millions of rows of meaningful, syntactically correct test data. This add-on module reads a database schema and displays database objects such as tables and columns; users can point, click, and specifically define how to populate the table.

Benchmark Factory® for Oracle

Benchmark Factory® for Oracle helps prevent unplanned downtime and slow performance by load-testing your system's limits using either industry-standard benchmarks or your own specified/captured transactional criteria before you go live with an Internet site, database, email system, or file server.

QDesigner™ Physical Architect

QDesigner™ Physical Architect is a database design and application tool that combines object-oriented, conceptual, and physical data object–modeling capabilities in a single, integrated environment. This add-on module has an intuitive user interface and provides support for more than 30 popular DBMSs.

Index

We'd like to hear your suggestions for improving our indexes. Send email to
index@oreilly.com.

CPSIA information can be obtained at www.ICGtesting.com
Printed in the USA
BVOW040546200812

298268BV00002B/4/P